NATIONAL TRUST
Book of Bread

NATIONAL TRUST
Book of Bread

Jane Eastoe

🍂 **National Trust**

First published in the United Kingdom in 2020 by
National Trust Books
43 Great Ormond Street
London WC1N 3HZ

An imprint of Pavilion Books Group Ltd

First published in the United Kingdom in 2014 under the title
Bread Making.

ISBN 9781911358886

A CIP catalogue for this book is available from the British Library.

10 9 8 7 6 5 4 3 2 1

Repro by Mission Productions Ltd, Hong Kong.
Printed and bound by Toppan Leefung Printing Ltd, China

This book can be ordered direct from the publisher at the website:
www.pavilionbooks.com, or try your local bookshop. Also available
at National Trust shops or www.nationaltrustbooks.co.uk

Contents

Introduction

We all appreciate the charms of a floury artisan loaf warm from the oven, a baguette fresh from a French bakery, a saffron bun purchased from a farmers' market in Cornwall, or the fantastic flavours of a dense wholemeal loaf made by a friend at home. Bread, although a dietary staple, is one of the world's great gourmet foods, and whilst the convenience of the shop-bought loaf cannot be denied, it bears very little resemblance to the charms of bread made by hand.

There is an apparent mystique to bread making that deters many people from having a stab at it, even though they would not think twice about knocking up a delicate soufflé, stuffing and roasting a goose, or using a blowtorch to caramelise the sugar on top of a crème brûlée. But bread making is no more complex than any of the culinary arts; indeed, the method is so simple that a child can knock up a loaf with ease.

Bread making appeals to very base instincts! Making a loaf is an intensely satisfying physical experience; turning a sticky mass of flour, water and yeast into a silky piece of dough, with a life of its own, is positively sensual. Seeing a piece of dough grow to twice its size never fails to thrill. And the smell of fresh baked bread alone is so positively intoxicating that estate agents maintain it can tip the balance in house purchases.

It is easy to become nostalgic about the lost art of bread making, to have visions of our ancestors kneading dough at the farmhouse table through a hazy, soft-focus cloud of flour. The truth is not so picturesque, for whilst bread has been integral to our survival – it has been a staple since the Stone Age – making it ourselves has not always been possible. Growing the grain to make flour, grinding it by hand, or taking it to the miller to be ground, is hard graft. Kneading bread at home may have been part of the daily routine, but often it was taken to a central oven to be baked as most people did not have the luxury of owning an oven in their home. Indeed, we have been dependent on bakers as far back as the early Egyptians and the Romans.

What has changed is that bread is no longer made locally, by skilled individuals using the same basic systems and ingredients as our forebears, to create fantastic, nutritious and tasty loaves. The Chorleywood mass production process, developed in 1961, intrinsically changed the nature of our daily bread. With the introduction of additives, and high-speed mixing, the natural rising and proving stages of bread making were curtailed, creating a cost-efficient loaf that was 40 per cent softer, more uniform in shape with a longer shelf life. This at the expense of taste, texture and nutrition. Today in Britain, we consume around 12 million loaves a day. Some 80 per cent of sales are made from the pre-packed loaves produced by large bakeries; in-store bakeries account for 17 per cent of sales, while just three per cent are taken by small high street bakers.

But the good news is that we are better equipped today to make delicious bread at home than ever before in history. The mass of bread-making flours for sale in the supermarkets are far superior to anything our forebears used. Heritage flours, made from blends of old varieties of wheat, can be purchased from traditional mills, specialist suppliers and over the internet. Many watermills and windmills are being restored to grind flour again. The National Trust is doing so in many places, from Cotehele in Cornwall to Hardwick in Derbyshire, often so they can grind home-grown wheat and bake on site or sell flour locally. Regional flour from all over the world can be bought locally, allowing us to make our own authentic versions of a range of foreign breads. Water comes out of the tap and we all have ovens in which to bake. Yeast is readily available, both fresh and dried, or we can make our own wild yeast from sourdough starters at home.

No excuse there then. Nor should time constraints be an issue. Bread making does not actually take much energy – just some short bursts of activity spread out over a matter of hours. Indeed, with our sedentary lives, you might like to look upon a little light kneading as ten minutes of exercise, though none could pretend that bread making is good for the waistline. Nevertheless, the more bread you make, the more you will make, and producing a loaf will become as much a part of the rhythm of life as brushing your teeth in the morning.

This book has a mass of recipes for you to try, some simpler than others and most steeped in history and tradition. You can enjoy making regional breads from Scotland, England, Ireland and Wales, as well as tackling historic recipes. I have also included some popular foreign breads, as well as a few contemporary recipes. You will quickly discover favourites that you can turn out in no time at all.

There is one simple truth about bread making – you never stop learning. I am not going to pretend that I am a master baker. I am merely an enthusiastic amateur and have had my fair share of disasters. I would urge you to read about the ingredients and processes of bread making before you get your pinny on so that my failures will help you to avoid the same pitfalls. Above all else, please, please do not let one small set-back deter you.

Nor should you let the lack of fancy equipment stop you from having a go. It is very helpful to have a bread cutter, a dough scraper and a banetton – of which more later. However you can manage perfectly well without these gadgets. None of the recipes in this book require the use of a mixer; I still don't have one myself and I get terribly cross when recipe books specify their use because I feel excluded.

So let's celebrate our national heritage, rediscover the joy of bread making and feed our families the kind of bread that makes them sigh with pleasure! I am not saying you will never buy another sliced loaf, but I am encouraging you to spread your culinary wings and start to make bread on a regular basis.

Ingredients

"*We were served on gold and silver plates, but we had to eat the same kind of war bread that every other family had to eat.*"
Eleanor Roosevelt, Buckingham Palace, 1942

Salt

I have decided to begin with salt because it's the ingredient that is easiest to forget. For this reason, I've put salt first in all the recipes in this book. In my opinion a loaf without salt does not taste good. But its function is more than just mere flavouring: salt tightens the gluten network and thus regulates the speed at which the dough rises. Without it, your dough may well be sticky and difficult to work. You can use regular table salt, but most serious bakers use rock salt or sea salt, although not the coarse granular form as these crystals don't incorporate so easily. Look for a fine-grain rock or sea salt if you want to make life easy, or attack your crystals with a pestle and mortar to reduce them to a fine grain. Salt inhibits the action of yeast and therefore it's really important to keep the two ingredients apart. Some purists argue that if you seek out traditionally milled flour to use in bread making it is so flavourful that the addition of salt is unnecessary.

Yeast

Yeast is a member of the *Saccaronmyces*, or 'sugar fungi'. As it breaks down the starches in flour into the sugar it needs for sustenance, it releases alcohol and carbon dioxide, and it is these gas bubbles that inflate and ferment the dough during rising, proving and the early stages of baking. The alcohol is lost as the dough is baked. When it is fed, the yeast will reproduce furiously – its cells will divide, and the process continues apace. The temperature of the dough needs to be between 25–30°C (77–86°F) for the yeast to be active. To put that in perspective, a comfortable room temperature for us is usually somewhere in the region of 18–20°C (64–68°F). A drop in temperature or a draught will inhibit the action of the yeast, which is why it is so important to maintain your dough at a steady temperature and keep it covered.

Fresh yeast and dried yeast can be substituted, as long as the appropriate methods are followed. As a rule of thumb, you usually require twice the weight of fresh yeast to dried yeast. In this book, I will give you the required weights for all types of yeasts, as when I started making bread I never seemed to have the correct yeast specified by the recipes.

Fresh Yeast
Fresh yeast can be obtained from many good organic shops as well as some supermarkets, or you may be able to purchase it direct from a supermarket bakery. It is sold in small blocks – you only need a little – and it has a short life of around two weeks. You must keep it in the refrigerator. Some people maintain that fresh yeast can be frozen successfully, but, in my experience, this is rather hit and miss.

Fast Action Dried Yeast and Dried Yeast
Dried yeast is available in two forms: dried yeast granules, which need to be activated with liquid, or fast-action (easy blend) granules, which are mixed directly into the dry ingredients. Fast-action yeast is easy to use, reliable and convenient – ideal for beginners. Be sure to keep it out of direct contact with salt as you add the ingredients. Dried yeast, like fresh, must be mixed with tepid water or milk, then left for 15–20 minutes until frothing, before it can be used.

Sourdough Starter

The good news is that some people who are gluten 'sensitive' may find that they can digest sourdough bread without any unpleasant side effects. The wild yeast and bacteria incubated in a starter help to break down the proteins and carbohydrates in the flour. For the

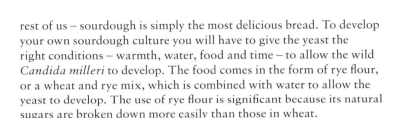

rest of us – sourdough is simply the most delicious bread. To develop your own sourdough culture you will have to give the yeast the right conditions – warmth, water, food and time – to allow the wild *Candida milleri* to develop. The food comes in the form of rye flour, or a wheat and rye mix, which is combined with water to allow the yeast to develop. The use of rye flour is significant because its natural sugars are broken down more easily than those in wheat.

You'll usually only use around a quarter of your starter at a time. Top it up when you remove some, so that you always have a starter to use. Once it is established, it will continue to develop and the flavour can become quite strong. Most people keep their starters in a fridge and just bring them up to room temperature before use. They can be frozen but lose some of their potency in the process. However, it is faster than starting the whole process from scratch.

A sourdough starter cannot be used interchangeably with any recipe, as with fresh yeast or dried yeast. A starter can be made with various flours (see page 114), which impact on the behaviour of the dough. Until you gain experience working with starters, it is best to follow a recipe for sourdough bread.

Raising Agents

Some breads, as well as many cakes, use raising agents instead of yeast. Bicarbonate of soda is alkaline and produces carbon dioxide as soon as it is mixed with an acidic substance, such as yoghurt, buttermilk or soured cream. The carbon dioxide gas forms bubbles in the dough, which expand when exposed to heat. The process is fast and the dough should be moved from the mixing stage to cooking as quickly as possible.

Flour

Almost anything can, and has been, ground into flour – wheat, obviously, but also rye, barley, spelt, corn, oats, rice, chestnuts, chickpeas, soya and even acorns have been used during times of famine. Theoretically, you can use any type of flour to make bread, but that doesn't mean you should reach for any old bag of flour as the resulting loaf may be of more use as a deadly weapon! Some grains, or combination of grains, are better for bread making than others, and these are characterised by their percentage of gluten content. Flour contains the proteins *gliadin* and *glutenin*. When they are mixed with water and oxygen, these bond together and form gluten. These chains of gluten lengthen as you knead the dough, and the more it is worked, the stretchier and more elastic it becomes. This elasticity gives the dough enough strength to expand and produce bread with a better structure.

Strong flour, which we use for bread, has a higher percentage of protein – between 12–15 per cent – than regular plain or self-raising flour, which has 8–10 per cent. Extra strong bread flour, as its name suggests, has even more protein – 15–16 per cent, and this tends to be utilised for making bagels and in some bread making machines. If you want to compare this with the 'soft' plain flour that most of us have in our cupboards, this has a gluten content of around 7–9 per cent and therefore it can't form sufficient elasticity to support the structure of the loaf.

Wheat
Wheat forms the basis of most bread flours. To understand why a loaf is white or brown it is essential that you understand the structure of wheat. The outer skin of the grain – or the wheat berry – is the bran, a fibre that contains protein. The wheatgerm is the embryo of new life (rather like the yolk of an egg) and is packed with vitamins. Finally, the endosperm, which makes up about 85 per cent of the grain, contains starches, sugars, minerals, proteins and oil. It is the combination of these parts of the grain that gives flour its character when milled. Traditional milling by stone crushes the grain between revolving stones – all the parts save the husk. This produces wholemeal or, as it is called in some countries, whole wheat flour. This is the most nutritional flour of all and is known as 100 per cent extraction.

The development of roller milling in the late nineteenth century made it easier to produce white flour than earlier sifting methods. Using this production method, wheat passes between steel cylinders, which remove the outer layers of the grain. Each part can then be utilised to produce various mixes of flour. Until recently it was then routinely bleached for aesthetic purposes but European legislation now prohibits this.

The various other brown mixes have an extraction rate of around 80 per cent and contain a percentage of white flour and wholemeal flour. For example, malted grain flours contain a blend of white and wholemeal flour combined with malted grains, which give the loaf a sweeter taste.

Different flour blends impact on the flavour and texture of the loaf, but the basic bread making technique remains the same whatever flour is used. It is worth noting that bread made with wholemeal flour needs a little more water in the mix, commonly 10–20 per cent more than white bread dough. This, however, requires slightly less kneading but takes longer to prove. The same is true for brown flour, which is usually a blend of wholemeal and other flours. You don't need me to point out that a wholemeal loaf will always be denser than a white loaf.

Flour Grades

Keen bakers seek out local mills, whose flour, milled using crops from the surrounding area, has its own distinctive flavour, which is quite different from the uniform flavour of commercially milled flour. It is these subtleties and variations that create such interesting loaves. By the same token, continental wheat flour contributes to the distinctive flavour and texture of the breads from those regions and accounts for the fact that although we can replicate bread recipes, they never taste *quite* the same or have the same crumb.

In Britain we commonly use hard/hard flour in bread, but you can also get the following gradations: hard/soft, soft/hard, and soft/soft, the latter being the kind of very fine flour that is used in cake making.

Our native wheat varieties are lower in gluten content and produce a loaf with a dense crumb – more like an Italian bread than what we traditionally associate with the UK. Most of our bread flours are a mix of Canadian or American wheat varieties (Hard Winter Red and Hard Spring Red) to improve the gluten content, combined with British grain for flavour. Organic flour producers are increasingly using heritage varieties of old English wheat, such as Maris Widgeon (also traditionally favoured by thatchers), to improve flavour.

Spelt is an ancient variety of wheat that was in common use from the Bronze Age. With its sweet, nutty flavour, it was much favoured by the Romans and was a staple food for peasants until the Middle Ages. Today it can be purchased as white or wholemeal flour and is very nutritious. The downside is that it produces a loaf with an unappetising grey hue. Spelt flour does not need as much kneading and proves quickly.

Italian bread flour has a higher starch content and is lower in protein than traditional strong flour. It is graded numerically: 00 flour is a white flour milled from durum wheat, whereas grade 04 is roughly equivalent to wholemeal. You can make perfectly nice Italian bread with strong white flour, but if you want it to be very authentic you should use 00 flour. It is lower in gluten and produces a nice crisp crust.

Rye

Rye features in many regional breads across Eastern Europe, Scandinavia and Russia because it grows in the kind of cold climates that defeat other crops. It was once a staple English grain and used to make maslin bread, but today it is mostly imported. The rye grain contains less gluten and therefore the dough will be less elastic and will produce a dense loaf structure and intense fruity flavour. You need to add more water to a rye dough or it will acquire the consistency of a household brick! The flour is sold as light or dark, depending on the amount of whole grain it contains. The darker the flour, the deeper the colour of the bread – light rye flour can produce a loaf with a distinctly grey crumb. Some people love it, but in my

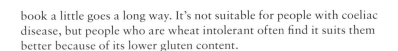

book a little goes a long way. It's not suitable for people with coeliac disease, but people who are wheat intolerant often find it suits them better because of its lower gluten content.

Barley
Barley has a mild and nutty flavour and contains more fibre than wheat. It has a lower gluten content – and, indeed, fewer calories – than wheat, so it is often combined with other strong flours to impart its nutritional qualities and flavour, usually in a ratio of one-quarter barley to three-quarters wheat. It is often used in flatbreads, and in Scotland for bannocks.

Oats
Oats thrive in cool, moist climates, which is why they do so well in Scotland and feature in so many of that country's regional dishes. Oats have to be dried in a kiln before grinding to remove the husk and reveal the groat. They are then ground to produce a variety of different grades, ranging from pin-head to super-fine. Rolled oats are made from pin-head oatmeal. Medium and fine oatmeal are most commonly utilised in bread making, notably in oatcakes but also bannock, which is a delicious unleavened flat bread.

Corn
Corn flour is derived from the endosperm of the corn kernel and is, as you doubtless know, used as a thickening agent, but not in bread. Cornmeal, however is utilised right across the world, notably wherever corn, or maize as it is known in the United States, grows readily. It comes in a variety of forms, depending on what parts of the kernel have been utilised. Cornmeal is milled from corn kernels and is not as fine as wheat flour. White cornmeal is used to make cornbread. In the United Kingdom, we use the word corn as a generic term to describe crops of any kind of grain – although perversely never to describe a field of maize.

Gluten-free Flour

Wheat is off limits in a gluten-free diet, as are barley and rye, so gluten-free flour utilises grains such as rice, tapioca, maize and often potato as its base ingredients. As it contains no gluten to form sticky elastic bonds and help the dough rise, plant gums are included in the flour to replicate the action of the gluten. These mixes tend to require rather more liquid than other loaves and therefore need a specially adapted recipe (see page 110).

Liquids

Liquids serve two purposes in bread making: to hydrate some types of yeast, and to bind all the dry ingredients together. Tap water, whether hard or soft, is fine for bread making, although some purists prefer to use bottled spring water.

Milk is also used, for it produces bread with a softer crust and crumb. Warmed milk is commonly used to hydrate and activate yeast as it accesses the sugars in it. The temperature is important; if you have a thermometer it should be touching around 38°C (100°F). If you don't own a thermometer, heat the milk to blood temperature – if it is too cold it won't activate the yeast, but if it is too hot it will kill it! Other breads utilise liquids such as apple juice, cider or beer.

Sugar

A small amount of sugar is a common ingredient in bread making – it helps to activate the yeast. It also features in sweet breads and makes the dough stickier and take longer to prove. White sugar is usually added to white bread mixes, whereas wholemeal blends may utilise brown sugar, honey or treacle.

Eggs

The addition of eggs makes the dough richer and softens bread. They also help a loaf to stay fresh for longer.

Fat

Vegetable oils – all culinary varieties – and animal fats, ranging from butter to lard, can be used in bread making. Fat has a softening effect, helps to keep bread fresh and imparts flavour. It also inhibits the action of the yeast, so dough with fat in it may well require a longer proving time.

Seeds, Grains, Nuts and Dried Fruit

These can add flavour and texture to bread as well as being utilised for decorative effect. A simple rule of thumb is less is more. Too many seeds can make your loaf hard to digest, so some recipes suggest that you soak them first to make them softer. However, this is not always the case, so do be guided by the recipe. Dried fruit will absorb moisture from your dough, so it is generally soaked before use.

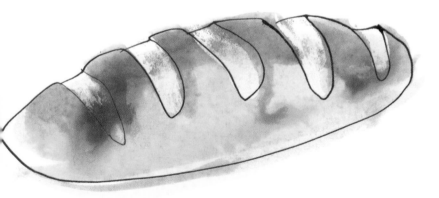

The Science and Stages
of Bread Making

○────────────○

"It is natural for sourness to make the dough ferment, and likewise that people who live off fermented bread having weaker bodies." Pliny the Elder

The number of people who think nothing of tackling complex and time-consuming cordon bleu recipes but who shy away from making their own bread is surprising. Time is the most often cited excuse, but the reality is that bread making doesn't take much time – rather short bursts of activity, interspersed with long stretches of doing nothing. All it takes is a little organisation. It is perhaps the many variables in bread making that people find daunting. The process is purely scientific, but it is not a precise science, and achieving a good end result is an art that is learned by experience. By feeling the dough, and learning when it is risen and proven, or when it is too wet or dry, we begin to grasp the finer points of the art. By mastering techniques in moulding and shaping a beautiful loaf, and by understanding how to detect precisely when it is perfectly cooked, we build our confidence. In making mistakes we learn, so don't give up if everything doesn't go perfectly to plan the first time you bake. Although, having said that, there is no reason why your first attempt should not produce perhaps the most delicious loaf of bread that you have ever tasted. And, take it from me, *nothing* tastes better than your first loaf of bread, unless, of course, you've forgotten to add the salt!

Your ultimate aim is to produce a loaf with a perfect 'crumb', the crumb being the term that bakers use to describe the inner construction of the loaf, that is the number of air holes within it. A loaf with a perfect crumb will have a light and even texture where the carbon dioxide bubbles have expanded properly in the rising process.

Equipment

It is very tempting when you first start bread making to rush out and purchase all manner of exotic equipment. The fact is that you can get by with very little if needs be. A loaf tin or two are useful, and digital scales are, in my book, essential. A large wooden board for kneading is invaluable – it's easier to take the board to the sink to clean than make repeated trips with a dishcloth to the table.

A raffia proving basket, or *banneton*, is lovely to own – although they can be horribly expensive for what they are, you can just use a kitchen bowl. Their function is to support heavier, wetter doughs as they are proving and to pattern them, producing concentric rings of the type you'll see in artisan bakeries. They are sometimes lined with linen, which produces a smooth loaf. If you are useful with a needle it is easy enough to make your own liner – a coarse linen produces a better effect than a fine one. Whichever form you opt for, flour it heavily before use and shake out the excess – this stops the dough from sticking.

Linen cloths can be useful for covering bread while proving. A large linen tea towel might do the job, although it may be a little on the small side.

A water spray bottle is cheap and easy to obtain and is used to spray over some loaves just before they go into the oven, to produce a crisper crust. I have been known to just flick water on with my fingers.

Baking bread on stones is the traditional way to bake bread, but baking stones are expensive – especially if they are large enough to be of real use. You can simply buy a suitably sized chunk of stone from a merchant, or use unglazed quarry tiles instead – glaze can contain lead, so glazed tiles are not recommended for this purpose. The stone, which should go into the oven at least five minutes before you start baking so that it is warm, will help with efficient heat transference and produce a better crust. However, an ordinary baking tray – the thicker the better – will be perfectly adequate.

It is lovely to own a peel – essentially a flat shovel – to allow you to quickly and easily transfer your dough onto and from your baking stone or tray. It will certainly help you to keep your perfectly shaped dough in pristine condition as it is transferred, but home bakers can manage perfectly well without this piece of equipment.

Griddles are used to cook some items quickly on a direct heat. Pikelets, crumpets, Welsh cakes and oatcakes all utilise this traditional method of cooking. If you don't have one, you can improvise with a heavy frying pan.

Measuring Out and Mixing

I cannot stress enough that measuring ingredients precisely is very important for novice bread makers – artisan bakers may be able to judge when their dough needs a little more flour or water, but it takes a lot of practice to become that skilled. If you buy only one piece of equipment, it should be digital scales.

Follow the recipe carefully when it comes to adding your yeast – there are three types of yeast you can use and they all need to be treated differently. Fast-action yeast can be added directly to the dry mix; fresh yeast and dried yeast will need hydrating first. Check your packaging carefully, so you are clear about what kind of yeast you are using.

Most ingredients are commonly mixed in all together and then kneaded – however, if you are adding dried fruit, olives, tomatoes or grains you will incorporate these when the dough has been worked sufficiently to be left to rise. The reason is simple: if you pummel and work soft items for 10 minutes they will be pulverised, and if you try to knead dough containing grains, it will hurt your hands.

Some recipes call for the dough to be mixed and worked without the yeast or salt being added – these are incorporated later in the kneading stage – so just follow your recipe.

Kneading

I cannot advocate the joy of kneading bread highly enough. It is a positively sensuous experience and wildly therapeutic as a means of relieving stress! You will learn that the dough gradually changes as you work it. At first it will stick to the table and your hands, gradually changing to become silky and pliable to the touch. There is no absolute technique; you will be kneading with your fists and stretching and folding the dough with your fingers and palms, for about 10 minutes – you might want to flour your hands lightly before you begin. Do not, whatever happens, be tempted to add any more flour to the dough because it is sticky; just keep working it and the texture will gradually change, becoming more elastic as you work and as the gluten bonds develop. The more bread you make, the easier it will be to tell when it is ready for proving. You might want to shape the dough into a round every so often. This doesn't serve any special purpose but it builds up your skills for later in the process.

A simple test to tell whether the dough has been kneaded sufficiently is to take a small piece and stretch it. You are aiming to be able to see light through it without it tearing. It's a useful exercise for beginners, allowing you to test how the process is progressing and to develop your ability to tell whether or not a dough has been kneaded enough just by feel.

It is possible to overwork dough, although it's quite hard to do this by hand. More commonly, it occurs when machines are left to do the work for you. Essentially the gluten structure, which you have worked so hard to develop, collapses and the dough reverts to being sticky and looks curdled – it is best to start again if this happens and chalk it up to experience.

When the dough is ready for proving this is the time to add any additional ingredients – stretch your dough out, scatter the extras over the top, then fold your dough over and knead just long enough to incorporate the ingredients evenly.

Finally, shape your loaf into a neat round, working it around and around gently between your hands until you have the required shape, whether circular or oval.

Rising

Dough is left to rise so that fermentation can take place and results in bread that is more flavourful and digestible. In the process of rising, gluten is stretched and softened by the action of the yeast and, over a period of time and given the right conditions, will double in size. You can pop it back into the bowl it was mixed in to rise – this must have enough capacity to contain it as it expands to twice its proportions.

You may be advised to flour the dough lightly, or to oil the bowl it will sit in – both these actions serve to help stop the dough drying out and make it easier to turn it out of the bowl at the end of its rise. For the same reason you will cover the top of the bowl with plastic, which also retains humidity and warmth and, importantly, keeps the dough draught free. You can use cling film or a shower cap (even a bin bag!); just make sure that there is plenty of room for the dough to grow like Topsy without touching the plastic – it'll stick like glue.

The dough should be left in a warm place to rise – but not too warm or it will rise too quickly. An airing cupboard is too warm, for example, as is anywhere near a cooker. Professionals like to prove their dough at temperatures of around 20–24°C (68–75°F). If it is not warm enough the dough will still rise but it may just take a little longer. You can put dough in the fridge to rise overnight if you don't have time to do everything in one go. You can also slow down the rising process by using less yeast. If the dough takes longer to rise it improves its flavour, but this is something to play with when you are more confident in your bread making abilities.

It is possible to leave dough to rise for too long, at which point it will start to sag a little and lose its elasticity. It's still OK to use, but the resulting loaf won't be quite as good.

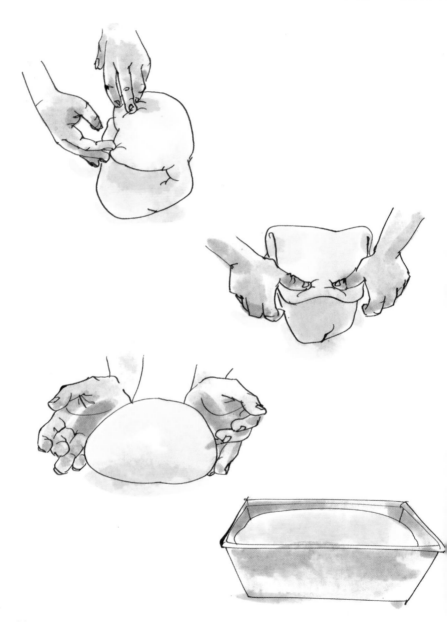

Knocking Back

Despite the term, don't be too aggressive with your dough in this stage. Press it with your fingertips – this will leave very satisfactory dents, until it has reduced to its original volume, or just knead by hand briefly and gently – not for more than about 15 seconds. Some types of dough are very wet – Italian breads for instance contain a lot of olive oil – and you may find it easier to gently stretch and fold them to reduce the volume of the dough.

Shaping

It is at this point that you shape your dough to enable it to 'grow' into the desired finished product. You might simply pop it into a loaf tin, or shape the same dough by hand to let it take on a natural appearance. You might work the dough into a couple of rounds to produce a traditional design, such as a cottage loaf, slashing the top, or utilise a proving basket for an artisan effect, or divide the dough into a number of rolls.

Shaping is an art that is learned with practice. Keep it simple to begin with and work your way up to more complex effects. Loaves can be any size but are usually no heavier than 800 grams. Baguette sticks weigh around 400 grams and rolls around 120 grams. Weigh your dough for accuracy when you are making rolls and you will get a uniform result.

If you are using a tin, stretch the dough until it is twice the length of your tin, flatten it, and fold it into three, placing it into the tin with the fold side underneath; it shouldn't be a snug fit and there should be room at each end for expansion.

White bread dough will expand more than wholemeal bread dough, so you may need to select your tin accordingly, and certainly don't think that because one type has risen more than the other it is a better loaf.

If you want to shape your loaf into a cob instead of using a loaf tin, use your hands to cup and shape the dough, turning it and tucking any ragged edges underneath until you have a smooth round. You'll find illustrations in the centre of the book showing the various bread shapes.

Oily bread, such as focaccia and ciabatta, are stretched and folded into shape. You may want to make dents in the surface with your fingers and pour some more oil over before baking.

Proving baskets do the work of shaping the dough for you. If the dough is very sticky, merely place it with the smooth side at the bottom, so that when it is inverted for baking it will have a lovely even top. If the dough is firmer, shape it before you place it in the basket.

If you want to add flour, grains or nuts as decoration, this is the point at which you do this. You don't have to use the same flour to dust the loaf as you did in its construction – simply drop a small handful of flour over the top of the loaf and roll it around so that it is coated all over. If you want to add nuts or seeds as decoration, just dip the top of the dough in a plate of milk or water, then dip it into a plate of seeds so that they will stick.

Proving

Proving your dough allows it to rise for a second time. It either sits in its tin, its proving basket, or on a floured board. A cloth can be folded up around the sides of the loaf to offer it a small degree of support as it rises – a method commonly used with baguettes when a number are proving at the same time. As with rising, the aim is for the dough to double in size, and this can take half an hour or a couple of hours – just keep an eye on it – you don't want it to over prove and start to sag. Remember that your dough will continue to rise in the oven – so when it comes to proving, always err on the side of caution.

Recipes often say 'leave your dough to rise until it reaches the top of the tin'. This is all very well, but tin sizes can be variable and we don't necessarily all own a full range of every conceivable size and shape of tin. How else can you tell if bread has risen sufficiently to be baked? Your fingers can provide you with one of the best tests. After the first rising and after you've knocked back your dough, shaped it, and placed it in its tin, press it gently with your fingertips – it will feel firm and you'll see that it will spring back into shape very quickly. The dough changes in consistency as it rises and feels spongier.

If you ignore all the indications that the dough is crying out to be baked, it will continue to produce carbon dioxide bubbles until the gluten network can no longer support the gas bubbles – at which point the dough begins to collapse. If you press it gently with your fingertips it will not spring back into shape.

Don't forget to turn your oven on while your loaf is proving; it must be up to temperature when the bread goes in. A recipe will usually give you some idea of how long the loaf is likely to need to prove, so always make sure you turn the oven on in plenty of time.

If you want to make slashes in your loaf, you should do this immediately before popping the dough into the oven when baking crusty loaves like bloomers and coburgs. However, when baking in a tin, make slashes in the early stages of the second proof. Slashes not only provide a traditional decoration, they also help the loaf to expand in the oven. The proving process leaves the dough in contact with the air, which dries it and slows rising. In making a cut you are exposing the soft stretchy dough to the heat and it will rise rapidly. Draw your knife – a serrated bread knife will suffice although you can get special blades – across the loaf to make a slash.

Baking

When the bread dough goes into a hot oven the yeast goes into overdrive and produces even more gas until the loaf reaches a temperature of around 55°C (131°F). The exterior cooks first, creating the crust, but the heat gradually works inwards until the centre is cooked and all the yeast is killed off. In the first five to ten minutes of baking the 'oven spring' occurs – this is when the bubbles of gas trapped in the dough are fully expanded and the starch in the outer layers of the bread is set – thus forming the crust, which will then brown.

Whether you are using a baking stone or baking tray, pop it into the oven a little while in advance to heat up. It will assist with the cooking process if it is pre-heated.

Professional bakers have ovens that can inject steam into them to create a crustier loaf. The steam condenses on the loaf, slowing the formation of the crust so that the loaf can expand for longer before the crust develops. If, like me and my children, you prefer a softer crust, then a lack of steam won't bother you. Many people advocate putting roasting tins containing freshly boiled water into the oven to replicate the effect; feel free to try this to see if you think it is worth the effort.

As a rough guide, a standard loaf will take approximately 30 minutes to bake, but ovens vary. The great question is: how can you tell if your loaf is cooked through? The common answer is that you tap it on the bottom and if it sounds hollow it's cooked. The problem I have with this theory is that I don't know what a hollow loaf should sound like and it all seems a little vague and theoretical. You will learn to judge by experience, but a sure fire method of telling if a loaf is fully cooked is to use a bread thermometer. You plunge this into your loaf; if you want a soft loaf and have utilised milk and fat it should be ready when the central temperature is around 85°C (185°F), or if you want a crustier loaf for sandwiches it should be ready when it has reached around 98°C (208°F). A good middle bet is 90°C (195°F). Please remember that fan assisted ovens cook food faster than conventional ovens, and at slightly different temperatures. You may need to experiment and adjust your timings accordingly. If you are concerned that the outside of your loaf is cooking much faster than the inside you can cover it up with a sheet of aluminium foil to help protect it.

When you remove your loaf from the oven take it out of its tin, or off its baking tray, as soon as possible – it will continue to cook until it is cooled – and place it on a wire cooling rack. You may be interested to know that once you have cooked your bread it is best stored wrapped in linen, or paper, in a bread-bin – the old-fashioned way. I know a lot of people keep bread in the refrigerator, but it actually dries out faster this way, plus home-made bread does not contain all the preservatives you'll find in shop-bought bread, so its shelf life will never compare favourably and nor should it. (Not that home-baked bread ever usually sits around for long enough to get stale.) However, if you have baked a number of loaves, do not forget that the freezer is a fantastic storage device – put the bread, sealed inside a plastic bag, into the freezer as soon as it has cooled – when you are ready to defrost it, it will take four to five hours to thaw fully.

Techniques

"For him a delicate loaf is reserved, white as snow and kneaded of the finest flour." Juvenal

A home-made loaf or pastry will taste stupendous no matter what it looks like. However, there are a set of techniques that will help you to produce a loaf that not only tastes good but looks spectacular, too. Most of the 'artwork' is done in the shaping stage, when the dough has been mixed, kneaded, knocked back and is being prepared for its final rise prior to being put into the oven. Some of the work is completed immediately before the loaf goes into the oven.

The first and simplest rule is to remember that whatever you are coaxing into shape is going to grow, and what you see now is not what you will get – your dough will bloom. It may take a leap of faith but those widely spaced balls of dough, or lumpen plaited strips of dough, will take on a life of their own. It's impressive, seriously impressive, and let's face it; we all like to dazzle our nearest and dearest on occasion. But it's not just the flashy shapes that are important – establishing the correct basic shape, dusting with different flours, or sprinkling with seeds or nuts, all help to make even the simplest loaf a thing of beauty.

Before shaping the dough, dust your hands with flour very lightly. Do not do this over the loaf, but to one side of it; you don't want to add any more flour to the bread, but you don't want it to stick to you either. What you are doing is creating a structure with a surface tension that will enable the dough to hold its shape as it rises.

The Shapes

A Round or Cob Loaf

Flatten the dough with your fingers and fold it over so you have a neat

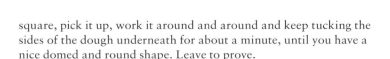

square, pick it up, work it around and around and keep tucking the
sides of the dough underneath for about a minute, until you have a
nice domed and round shape. Leave to prove.

Cottage Loaf

Divide the dough into two pieces, one twice the size of the other.
Shape into two rounds, using the technique above, then place the
smaller piece, centrally, on top of the larger piece of dough. Push a
thin rolling pin, or a wooden spoon, through the middle to make
a central hole. Leave to prove.

You can make an even more exotic version of this if, after leaving
the loaf to prove, you make slashes from top to bottom, at regularly
spaced intervals, around the sides.

Bloomer

Flatten the dough with your fingers and roll it up like a Swiss roll,
then flatten it out using the palm of your hand. Roll it up once again,
tucking the ends underneath. Leave it to prove and, just before
baking, make diagonal slits across the top with a sharp knife and
glaze with beaten egg, or a salt and water solution.

Baton

Flatten the dough by prodding it with your fingers to form a rough
circle, then fold the dough over in the middle – you can press a line
along the centre to make this easier. Tuck the two corners into the fold
at an angle. Press down along the fold to close it, and turn the dough
over so that the fold is underneath. Now keeping the dough on the
table, rock it back and forth in-between your hands, working along
the length and back again if necessary until it is a smooth oval. Leave
to prove.

If you want more of a cylindrical shape, which you see in so many
foreign breads, the basic technique is the same: Flatten the dough
with your fingers to form a circle, and then fold the dough over in
the middle – you can press a line along the centre to make this easier.
Stretch it out to twice its length, and then fold it into three. Flatten it

out again into a square with your fingers. Then roll it up tightly and press the join with your fingers to seal it. Leave to prove with the fold side down.

Crown

This is a very pretty effect and can be used for both bread and brioche dough. Divide the dough into nine pieces, one slightly larger than the rest. Shape into rounds and place, evenly spaced, in a round tin, with the larger piece in the centre. Leave to prove. Just before it goes into the oven glaze the dough by brushing it with a beaten egg and milk. This will grow into a fabulous domed sculpture that can, conveniently, be torn apart in nine easy pieces.

Tin Loaf

Flatten the dough by prodding with your fingers. You are aiming to get the following dimensions: the width of the dough should be equivalent to the length of the tin; and the length of the dough should be a little longer than the length of the tin. Roll the dough up towards you, as tightly as possible. Press the joint with your fingers to seal the seam. Place the dough so that the seam is underneath, and tuck the ends underneath, too. Lift the dough up and drop it into the tin. Leave to prove.

Plait

Divide the dough into three, and shape into three long rolls, each about 30cm (12in) long. Pinch the ends together at one end and make a loose plait, crossing each strand one over the other in turn. When complete, pinch this end together. If you prefer, you can start plaiting in the middle and work out to each end. Leave the dough to prove on a baking tray, or in a large loaf tin if you want a more contained effect. You might like to glaze the dough, by brushing it with a beaten egg and milk glaze, immediately before it goes into the oven and perhaps sprinkle it with poppy seeds.

There are also more complex plaited loaves you can make, with four, five, six and eight strands, but I believe in keeping life simple, and a plain three-strand plaited loaf is a thing of beauty.

Baguettes

It's hard to make a perfect baguette, but if you decide to have a crack at it, this is the way to shape one. Weigh the dough first; you want each baguette to weigh around 250g (9oz). Press each piece into a rectangle by prodding it with your fingertips. Roll the shortest side towards the centre, and keep working until you have a log shape. Place the join underneath and leave to prove for 20–30 minutes.

Remove the gas from the dough by gently prodding with your fingertips – you don't want to flatten it, just even out the consistency. Repeat the same rolling process, but this time put some pressure along the length of the seam to seal it. Gently roll the dough, as you used to roll plasticine as a child, ideally until it is about 35cm (14in) in length, but you may have to compromise length to get them to fit in the oven. Gently place the lengths of dough on a linen cloth, leaving spaces in between so that you can pull the linen up in pleats, on either side of the dough, to support it as it rises. Cover with plastic and leave them to prove for 45–60 minutes.

Transferring these lengths of dough to a tray is an art in itself – anything smooth and very thin will be of assistance, so this is where a peel comes into its own. Score the loaf with three to five shallow diagonal crossway cuts that overlap, then bake in the oven.

Rolls

You are aiming to get evenly sized rolls, whatever shape you want, with each piece of dough weighing between 100–150g (3½–5oz). A roll is simply a mini-loaf, so select which shape you want – round or oblong – and roll, using the same methods cited above. Making a batch of rolls is a good way to rapidly hone shaping techniques.

You could try your hand at making a knotted roll. Simply measure the dough out as before, then roll each piece into a thin sausage and tie in a knot. Leave to prove. Twisted rolls are equally simple to create; divide each piece of dough into two and roll into thin sausages. Hold both sausages together at one end and twist, then tuck the ends underneath and leave to prove.

Danish Pastries

A fiendishly fiddly dough to make, and twiddly to shape, nevertheless everyone loves a Danish and these creations really are an act of love.

Crescents

The same principles are used as for shaping a croissant; roll the dough out thinly and cut into two large circles, approximately 23–30cm (9–12in) in diameter. Divide each circle into eight segments, and pop a little almond paste, or whatever soft flavouring you are using, on the outside edge. Roll up the shape from the outer edge towards the point. Then curl it to form a crescent shape. Leave to prove for about 20–30 minutes.

Imperial Stars

Roll out the dough and cut it into squares of around 10cm (4in). Make diagonal cuts from each corner, stopping around 1.5cm (½in) short of the centre. Pop some almond paste into the middle, or a filling of your choice, then fold one corner of each section into the centre, where it will, hopefully, remain in place. If not, brush on a little beaten egg to help things stick together. Leave to prove for about 20–30 minutes.

Cushions

Once again roll out the dough and cut into squares of around 10cm (4in). Place some almond paste in the centre of each square, or fill as desired, and fold alternate corners into the centre. If necessary, secure the corners with a little beaten egg. Leave to prove for about 20–30 minutes.

Pinwheels

This is possibly the simplest shape to make. Roll out the dough into a rectangle. Spread the centre with your filling of choice – cinnamon butter and sultanas are a classic flavour – then roll the dough up into sausage and cut into slices of about 2.5cm (1in). Place, cut-side upwards, on a baking sheet. Leave to prove for about 20–30 minutes.

Recipes

○━━━━━━━━━━━━━━━○

"Rye and barley bread are looked upon with horror even by poor cottagers." Arthur Young, 1767

Before you start

Measurements

All the recipes in this book require some small precise measurements. If you do not have digital scales, please use proper measuring spoons to get an accurate weight – your mother's tablespoon from the cutlery drawer will not necessarily equate in either weight or volume to the precise given quantity.

For reference

1 tablespoon (tbsp) is 15ml

1 dessertspoon (dsp) is 10ml

½ tablespoon is 7ml

1 teaspoon (tsp) is 5ml

½ teaspoon is 2.5ml

¼ teaspoon is 1.25ml

Temperatures

There is a daunting emphasis on temperatures in bread making. Please don't be too alarmed by this. If a liquid is described as tepid it should feel at a comfortable bath temperature when you pop your finger into it. Always err on the side of caution; a liquid that is too hot can kill off yeast. If it is on the cool side it will only slow the process down a little. Where exactly is that 'warm place' that is mentioned so often? An airing cupboard is usually too warm, just do your best to find a spot that best fits the bill.

Room temperatures are variable throughout the year as well as from house to house. A cooler room will slow down the rising process, but it won't stop it altogether – things may just take a little longer. Dough can be put in the refrigerator overnight and it will still rise; it will just take longer.

Similarly oven temperatures cannot be relied upon to be absolutely accurate. Learn to trust your judgement and adjust temperatures and timings accordingly.

Yeast

If you have not yet read page 10 to familiarise yourself with the differences between the three main types of yeast before you begin I urge you to do so now. I favour using fast-action yeast because it is so reliable and easy, but you can use any kind of yeast in the recipes below, and I list the different weights required for both fast-action yeast and fresh yeast in each recipe.

However I have not included the method required for using fresh yeast in every single recipe, but you follow the basic rules below you can utilise any yeast you choose.

Both fresh yeast and basic dried yeast must be activated before they can be used, whereas fast-action yeast can simply be added to the dry ingredients.

If you wish to use fresh yeast or dried yeast instead of fast-action yeast, simply use a little of the liquid specified in the recipe to hydrate it. This activated yeast should be added to the dry ingredients when the liquid ingredient – be it milk or water – is called for in the method.

Fresh yeast is hydrated with a little liquid, and then left for 15–20 minutes until it starts to froth. The addition of a little sugar also helps this process along. Please note that twice the quantity of fresh yeast is used to a measure of dried yeast.

Similarly, basic dried yeast needs to be activated by a liquid and then left for 15–20 minutes until it starts to froth. As a rule of thumb, you use around the same quantity of basic dried yeast in a recipe as you would fast-action yeast.

Quick Breads

Soda Bread

Soda bread is the ultimate quick bread and a fantastic starter bread for beginners – especially when you've not got all the ingredients together for serious bread making. It's absolutely delicious, but doesn't keep for long, so make it when there's lots of people around to eat it all up in one sitting! You don't use bread flour, but common or garden white or wholemeal flour.

2.5g (½ tsp) salt
450g (1lb) wholemeal flour, or plain
   white flour, or a mixture
4g (1 tsp) sugar
4g (1 tsp) bicarbonate of soda
400ml (14 fl oz) buttermilk
OPTIONAL
A little milk if the mix is dry

Pre-heat the oven to 200°C (400°F), gas mark 6. Lightly flour a baking sheet.

Sift the dry ingredients into a bowl, then add the buttermilk and mix the ingredients together lightly. Feel free to use your hands.

Put the dough onto a lightly floured board and knead briefly – a minute should be more than enough. Shape it into a nice round and put it onto the tray. Cut a deep cross into it. The dough won't cook through if you don't almost cut through it.

Pop it into the oven and bake for about 40–45 minutes. I've undercooked soda bread a few times, usually because the cuts are too shallow, and it's not nice.

Soda Farls

The ingredients and method are the same as for soda bread, but farls are rolled out thinly and cooked on direct heat, instead of being baked in the oven. They are seriously yummy eaten hot and perfect with a fry-up at breakfast. If you are feeling decadent, spread them with butter!

2.5g (½ tsp) salt
450g (1lb) wholemeal flour, or plain
   white flour, or a mixture
4g (1 tsp) sugar
4g (1 tsp) bicarbonate of soda
400ml (14 fl oz) buttermilk
OPTIONAL
A little milk if the mix is dry

Prepare and knead the dough as on page 40.

Shape it into two rounds and roll them out in a circular or square shape, until about 1cm (½in) thick. Cut the circles into quarters, or, if you have opted for a square shape, cut it from corner to corner, so that you have eight triangles.

If you have a griddle, use it; if not, heat a non-stick frying pan until hot, dust lightly with flour, then dry-fry the soda farls, in batches, for around three minutes on each side, until golden brown.

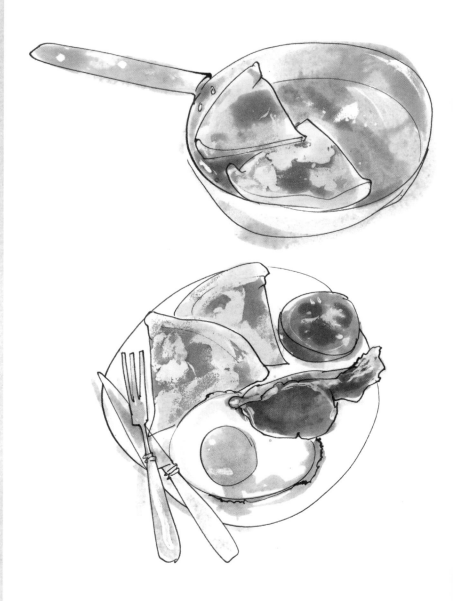

Potato Farls

These are naughty but nice in a savoury way! Again, absolutely divine with a full English breakfast!

A good pinch of salt
450g (1lb) potatoes
50g (2oz) butter
Freshly ground black pepper

50g (2oz) plain flour, plus a little extra
   for dusting
OPTIONAL
A little milk or cream

Peel the potatoes and cut them into pieces. Put into a saucepan of salted water and boil until cooked.

Drain, then return to the pan, add the butter, season with salt and pepper, and mash with a vengeance, until all the lumps have gone and the mash is lovely and soft – you might want to add a little cream or milk to make them nice and fluffy.

Add the flour and fold the mixture together. Turn out the mixture onto a lightly floured board and knead gently until you have a smooth dough. Roll this out – you are aiming for a circle – until it is 1cm (½in) thick. Cut the circle into four quarters.

Heat a griddle or non-stick frying pan until hot, dust with flour and dry-fry the potato farls for around three minutes on each side, until golden brown.

Basic Breads

Old-Fashioned Cottage Loaf

This old Cornish recipe comes courtesy of Jo Burgess of Tintagel Old Post Office, a National Trust property where they make the most of their Victorian cloam oven. Fires were made in the base of these masonry ovens, often built into the chimney, and then the ashes were raked out and bread or meat was cooked.

10g (2 tsp) salt
7g (2¼ tsp) fast-action dried yeast or
    15g (½oz) fresh yeast
1 tsp honey, if using fresh yeast
450ml (16 fl oz) hand-hot water

700g (1lb 8oz) strong white bread
    flour
25g (1oz) butter
OPTIONAL
1 beaten egg, to glaze

If you are using fresh yeast, put it into a bowl containing a quarter of the water and the honey, and mix together. Set aside until needed. Put the flour and salt into a large bowl, cut the butter into small pieces and rub it in. If you are using fast-action yeast just add it to the flour. Pour the water into the flour and mix well until all the ingredients are combined. You can use your hands from the start, or, if you prefer, start with a spoon and then use your hands once the ingredients have begun to come together.

Next is the kneading. I like to work off a large wooden board, but you can knead anywhere that suits you. However, it is very important to pick somewhere you can work at a comfortable height – if the surface is too low you may find that your back starts to ache after kneading for a while.

Turn the dough onto an unfloured surface and knead for 10 minutes until it begins to get silky and smooth to the touch. Please don't be tempted to add any more flour, as this will make the dough dry –

have faith that the dough will become less sticky as you continue to knead it.

Place the dough in a bowl. Cover with a plastic bag or use cling film if there is room for the dough to double in size. Leave the bowl in a warm place for about 1½–2 hours until it has doubled in size.

When the dough has risen sufficiently, knock it back gently to expel the air.

You can simply bake this as one piece on a greased baking tray, or, if you prefer to make it the traditional way, cut about one-quarter of the dough out and then shape both pieces into rounds. Place the larger circle onto a large greased baking tray and place the other on top. Using the end of a pointed rolling pin, make a hole through the centre.

Cover with a plastic bag and leave to prove for about 45 minutes to one hour.

Pre-heat the oven to 230°C (450°F), gas mark 8. Glaze the top of the loaf with some beaten egg and leave to prove for another 5–10 minutes.

Bake for 15 minutes at the high oven temperature, then lower it to 200°C (400°F), gas mark 6 and continue baking for approximately 20 minutes.

Transfer the loaf onto a wire rack and leave to cool.

Lady Hilaria's Wholemeal Loaf

Lady Hilaria Gibbs, daughter of the sixth earl of Edgcumbe, grew up in Cotehele, which had belonged to the Edgcumbe family since 1353. It was passed to the National Trust in 1947 on the death of her father, in lieu of death duties. Despite her privileged upbringing, Lady Hilaria could bake a fabulous loaf. This is her recipe, which is absolutely delicious, a pleasure to make and to eat!

7g (2¼ tsp) salt
250g (9oz) stoneground wholemeal
    flour
150g (5oz) strong white flour
25g (1oz) butter or margarine
10g (3¼ tsp) fast-action dried yeast
    or 20g (¾oz) fresh yeast

4g (1 tsp) brown sugar
15g (1 tbsp) oat bran
1 tsp black treacle
250ml (9 fl oz) warm water
A little milk for glazing
OPTIONAL
Sesame seeds for topping

Put the salt and flours into a mixing bowl, rub in the fat, then add the yeast, sugar and bran, and mix together well. Stir the treacle into the warm water, mix together, then add to the dry ingredients and bring together into a dough.

Knead for 10 minutes until smooth. Put the dough into a greased loaf tin, cover with a plastic bag or cling film, and leave to prove until doubled in size, about 1 hour.

Pre-heat the oven to 190°C (375°), gas mark 5.

Brush the top with milk and sprinkle with sesame seeds in the last 10 minutes of proving. Cook for 25–30 minutes until the loaf is golden brown. Cool on a wire rack.

Barley Bread

This is a seventeenth-century recipe from the National Trust's
Moseley Old Hall and was compiled by Monica Harthill,
with some adjustments for contemporary taste. It's dense and
flavoursome – anyone who tries it asks for the recipe.

7g (2¼ tsp) salt
550g (1lb 4oz) strong wholemeal flour
225g (8oz) barley flour
25g (1oz) rice flour

7g (2¼ tsp) fast-action dried yeast or
   15g (½oz) fresh yeast
70ml (2½ fl oz) brown ale
Around 350ml (12 fl oz) warm water
2 tsp clear honey

Mix all the dry ingredients in a warm bowl; if you are using fast-action yeast, add it now. If you are using fresh yeast, blend it to a cream with a little of the ale and put on one side for 15 minutes to activate it.

Combine the ale, the warm water and the honey. Stir this mixture into the dry ingredients and mix to a firm dough, adding a little extra water if necessary.

Knead for 10–15 minutes, until the dough feels soft and elastic. Shape into a ball and put into a lightly oiled bowl, then cover with a plastic bag and leave in a warm place until the dough has doubled in size.

Pre-heat the oven to Cook at 230°C (450°F), gas mark 8.

Knock back lightly and divide into two equal pieces.

Place in two 450g (1lb) bread tins.

Cover the dough with plastic bags and leave for 1–2 hours until well risen.

Cook for 20–25 minutes.

If the loaves are not quite cooked, you can cover them with aluminium foil and cook them for a little longer.

Cool on a wire rack and do not cut until cold.

Rye Bread

Rye bread is best left for 24–48 hours before eating and it keeps for days. It's very wet when first baked, so don't be surprised at the consistency of the crumb. It's fabulous toasted, very satisfying when you are hungry and glorious sliced wafer-thin and served with smoked salmon. This recipe is really simple and no real kneading is required.

5g (1 tsp) salt
300g (10½oz) light or dark rye flour
    (according to taste preference)
2.5g (¾ tsp) fast-action dried yeast or
    5g fresh yeast
250ml (9 fl oz) tepid water

If you are using fast-action yeast, simply put all the dry ingredients in a bowl, stir together, and then add the water. If you are using fresh yeast, mix it to a paste with some of the water before you begin and then incorporate as above with the rest of the water.

Pull the ingredients together to form a soft dough but do not knead. Grease a 450g (1lb) loaf tin, put the dough in and cover with a shower cap or plastic bag. Leave to rise in a warm place for about 2–4 hours.

Pre-heat the oven to 200°C (400°F), gas mark 6.

When the dough has risen, dust the top lightly with flour, and put the tin into the oven for 45–50 minutes.

Turn the loaf out of its tin and leave to cool, wrapped in a linen cloth.

Flowerpot Granary Loaf

This recipe is from Jo Burgess at the Tintagel Old Post Office. It looks incredibly pretty cooked and tastes splendid, too!

5g (1 tsp) salt

225g (8oz) strong white bread flour

225g (8oz) malted granary bread flour

5g (1¼ tsp) caster sugar

7g (2¼ tsp) fast-action dried yeast or
   15g (½oz) fresh yeast

150ml (¼ pint) warm milk

1 beaten egg, plus extra for glazing

15ml (1 tbsp) olive oil

100–150ml (3½–5 fl oz) warm water

Poppy and sesame seeds for topping

To begin with, you will need to prepare your flowerpot – use a classic terracotta pot shape that will hold around 1200ml (2 pints) of liquid.

Soak it in cold water for 30 minutes, dry thoroughly and brush the inside with oil.

Line with baking parchment, allowing the paper to come up over the edge of the pot as the dough may rise above the lip.

Mix the flours and salt in a large bowl, then stir in the sugar and yeast.

Pour in the warm milk, beaten egg, olive oil and enough warm water to form a soft wet dough.

Knead the dough on a lightly floured surface for 10 minutes until soft and smooth.

Place the dough in a lightly oiled bowl, cover with a plastic bag and leave it to rise in a warm place until doubled in size.

Knock back gently, then shape the dough into a smooth round with a roughly pointed end, so that it half-fills the pot.

Leave it until doubled in size.

Pre-heat the oven to 190°C (375°F), gas mark 5.

Brush the top of the bread with beaten egg, and sprinkle with poppy and sesame seeds. Bake as one large loaf for 45–50 minutes, or two small loaves for 15–20 minutes. Leave in the flowerpot to cool for 5–10 minutes, then place on a wire rack.

Cotehele Mill Maslin Bread

This splendid recipe comes from the National Trust's Cotehele Mill in Cornwall, which has been grinding flour since Tudor times. Maslin bread is dense and delicious; it was a staple food for labourers and servants. I am passionate about it toasted.

5g (1 tsp) salt
170g (6oz) stoneground wholemeal
   flour
100g (3½oz) rye flour
50g (2oz) barley flour
5g (1¾ tsp) fast-action dried yeast or
   10g (⅓oz) fresh yeast
250ml (9 fl oz) tepid water

Place all the dry ingredients in a bowl, add the water and bring together to form a dough.

Turn out onto a board and knead for 10 minutes; it's a very wet and sticky dough. Pop it back into the bowl, cover and leave to rise for 2–3 hours, until the dough has doubled in size.

Turn the dough back out onto the board and knock back lightly. Shape into a round or oblong loaf, place on a baking tray, cut a cross in the top, cover with a plastic bag and leave to rise for about an hour, until doubled in size.

Pre-heat the oven to 220°C (430°F), gas mark 8. Bake for about 25 minutes, until the loaf is cooked. Place on a wire rack to cool.

Fancy Breads

Milk Loaf

This is not so much fancy but wonderfully soft. Children love it, especially the rolls.

10g (2 tsp) salt
450g (1lb) strong white bread flour
8g (2 tsp) sugar
7g (2 ¼ tsp) fast-action dried yeast or

15g (½oz) fresh yeast
300ml (½ pint) tepid milk
50g (2oz) butter

If you are using fresh yeast, put it into a bowl with a little of the warm milk, stir it and put it on one side for 10–15 minutes to ferment, then add the rest of the milk.

Put the flour in a large mixing bowl and add the butter, cut into small pieces, and rub it in with your fingertips.

Add the sugar and salt. If using dried yeast, add it now.

Add the warm milk and mix together.

Tip it out onto a wooden board and knead for 15 minutes until soft.

Put it into a bowl, cover with a plastic bag and leave to prove for 1–2 hours, until it has doubled in size.

You can use this to make a loaf or rolls. Either way, knock back lightly and then put it into a lightly greased 1kg (2lbs) loaf tin or divide into 12–15 rolls and place on a lightly greased baking sheet.

Cover with a plastic bag and leave to double in size; this takes around 30 minutes to an hour.

Pre-heat the oven to 200°C (400°F), gas mark 6.

If you are baking rolls, cook them for about 15 minutes, then put them on a wire tray and cover with a linen cloth, so that their crust stays nice and soft.

If you are baking a loaf, put the tin in the oven and, after 20 minutes, turn it round, so it bakes evenly. Cook for a further 15–20 minutes.

Turn out onto a wire tray as soon as it comes out of the oven and cover with a linen cloth.

Crumpets

5g (1 tsp) salt
350g (12oz) strong white bread flour
7g (2¼ tsp) fast-action dried yeast or
   15g (½oz) fresh yeast

300ml (½ pint) tepid water
200ml (⅓ pint) tepid milk
2g (½ tsp) bicarbonate of soda
Oil for greasing

If you are using fresh yeast or dried yeast, put it in a bowl with half of the flour and the warm water, and beat until smooth. Cover and leave for some 20 minutes, until frothing. Then gradually add the other ingredients.

If you are using fast-action yeast, mix all of the dry ingredients together, then gradually add the warm water and milk, but keep a little milk back as you may not need to use it all. Beat it until you have a smooth batter, then put it on one side for about an hour, until the mixture rises and is full of bubbles.

Grease the frying pan and the inside of the crumpet rings. Put them into the frying pan and heat it up. When it's hot, add 2 tablespoons of the mixture to each crumpet ring – they should be about half full. Cook on a medium-to-low heat for about 10 minutes – until the surface has lots of holes and has dried out. The crumpets will shrink away from the sides of the ring as they cook, so they should slip out easily – but remember that those rings will be hot. Flip the crumpets over to cook for a few seconds on the other side to brown the tops. This recipe makes about 15 crumpets.

Serve the crumpets warm with lashings of butter!

English Muffins

5g (1 tsp) salt
450g (1lb) strong white bread flour
4g (1 tsp) sugar

7g (2¼ tsp) fast-action dried yeast or
  15g (½oz) fresh yeast
300ml (½ pint) tepid water

If you are using fresh yeast, mix it with the sugar and water and leave to ferment.

If you are using fast-action yeast, mix all the dry ingredients together in a bowl. Add the liquid to the dry ingredients and mix together.

Turn out the dough onto a lightly floured surface and knead for 10 minutes until smooth.

Put into a bowl, cover with a plastic bag and leave to rise in a warm place until doubled in size.

Knock the dough back gently and put it back in the bowl to rest for 5 minutes.

Place the dough on a lightly floured surface, then roll it out until it is 1cm (½in) thick. Don't be tempted to roll it out any thinner than this or your muffins won't have that wonderful density. However, if they're too much thicker, they will have to be cooked for longer.

Cover with a linen cloth and leave to rest for 5 minutes.

Take a 9cm (3½in) round cutter and cut the dough into between 8 and 12 muffins, depending on how large or small you like your muffins to be in diameter.

Lightly flour a baking sheet, put the muffins on top, dust the tops lightly with sieved flour or semolina. Cover with a plastic bag and leave to rise in a warm place until doubled in size – approximately 30 minutes.

Pre-heat the oven to 230°C (450°F), gas mark 8.

Bake the muffins for 5 minutes, then turn them over and bake for a further 5 minutes.

Eat fresh from the oven, or toasted.

You can also cook them on a griddle or a heavy-based frying pan, again for 5 minutes each side.

Pikelets

10g (2 tsp) salt
450g (1lb) strong white bread flour
5g (1 tsp) fast-action dried yeast or
   10g (⅓oz) fresh yeast

2g (½ tsp) bicarbonate of soda
300ml (½ pint) milk
300–350ml (10–12 fl oz) water
30ml (2 tbsp) vegetable oil

Mix all the dry ingredients together. Warm the milk, water and oil to blood heat. If you are using fresh yeast, add it to a little of the warm liquid and leave for 15 minutes. Then add the warm liquid to the dry ingredients and work it into a smooth batter.

Cover the bowl with some cling film and leave it to rise for 1½–2 hours, until it is bubbling and well risen.

Knock it back gently with a spoon, then cover it again with cling film and leave it to rise in a warm place for 30 minutes.

Take your griddle, grease it lightly with a little oil and heat it. Put a spoonful of the mix onto the griddle; you'll need to cook one at a time and do a dummy run to see how quickly it cooks and how much mix you need to use. Traditionally, pikelets are around 15cm (6in) across. The holes will appear almost straight away. Cook both sides until the pikelets are pale brown in colour. If the batter is too thick, you will end up with pikelets that are burned black on the outside and raw on the inside!

Malt Loaf

5g (1 tsp) salt
450g (1lb) plain white flour
350ml (12 fl oz) tepid water
14g (1½ tbsp) fast-action dried yeast
   or 25g (1oz) fresh yeast
45ml (3 tbsp) malt extract

30ml (2 tbsp) black treacle
25g (1oz) butter
225g (8oz) sultanas
SUGAR GLAZE
15g (1 tbsp) sugar
15ml (1 tbsp) water

Grease a 450g (1lb) loaf tin. If using fresh yeast, blend it with the water and put aside for 15 minutes until it is frothy. Sift the flour and salt into a bowl. If you are using fast-action yeast add it to these dry ingredients. Warm the malt extract, treacle and butter in a saucepan until just melted. Add the malt mixture and yeast liquid to the flour and mix well. Add the sultanas and mix the ingredients together for about 5 minutes. I use my hands – it's sticky, but it's easier than mixing the ingredients with a spoon.

Put the mixture into the tin. Cover with cling film and leave on one side for about 45 minutes, by which time the mixture, if it is in the correct size tin, should have risen to the top.

Pre-heat the oven to 200°C (400°F), gas mark 6. Bake for 40–45 minutes. Take the loaf out of the oven when cooked and leave to cool in the tin. Boil the sugar and water together to make a sugar glaze and brush this over the loaf while it's still warm.

Chelsea Buns

The Chelsea Bun House in Pimlico apparently did a roaring
trade in these enriched dough buns for a century. Filled with fruit
and covered in a honey glaze, they were reputedly a favourite of
both George II and George III before the Bun House burned down
in 1839.

3g (½ tsp) salt
225g (8 oz) strong white bread flour
7g (2¼ tsp) fast-action dried yeast or
   15g (½oz) fresh yeast
15g (½oz) butter
110ml (4 fl oz) tepid milk
1 egg, beaten
25g (1oz) melted butter
50g (2oz) soft brown sugar

100g (3½oz) mixed dried fruit, e.g.
   currants/sultanas/cranberries/
   raisins
Grated rind of 1 unwaxed lemon
GLAZE
15g (1 level tbsp) sugar
15ml (1 tbsp) water
Alternatively, melt a little jam or
   honey to brush the tops

Traditionally, Chelsea buns are made in a square cake tin. You are
aiming to produce a square bun with a round spiral, but a round tin
will do just as well for this purpose and the end result will taste every
bit as good. Grease an 18–20cm (7–8in) cake tin.

If you are using fresh yeast, mix together the tepid milk, yeast and 50g
(2oz) of the flour in a bowl and put on one side for 20 minutes, until it
is frothy.

Put the flour and salt in a bowl and rub in the 15g (½oz) butter. If
you are using fast-action dried yeast, add it now. Add the liquid and
beaten egg, and mix the ingredients together. Turn out onto a board
and knead for about 5 minutes, until you have a lovely satiny soft
dough – it will start off a bit sticky, but the end result feels wonderful.

Make it into a neat round, then pop it into a bowl and cover with plastic. Leave to rise until doubled in size – this takes about an hour.

When the dough is ready, turn it out onto a board and give it a gentle knead, then roll it out with a rolling pin until it is approximately 30 x 23cm (12 x 9in). You will have to work at this as the dough is very elastic and it will keep shrinking back. Brush the top with melted butter, then sprinkle the sugar, mixed dried fruit and lemon rind over the surface. Just keep the fruit and sugar approximately 2–3cm (1in) away from one of the long edges. Roll up the dough into a tight sausage, pinching along the join to help keep it together. Then cut into 8–9 pieces. Pop these into the cake tin and arrange nicely, so that when they rise they will all squidge together. If you have any melted butter left over, pour this over the top.

Pop this into a plastic bag and put on one side to rise until doubled in size – anything from 30–60 minutes. Pre-heat the oven to 190°C (375°F), gas mark 5, and cook the buns for about 25–30 minutes – keep an eye on them towards the end, as you don't want them to burn. While they are warm, brush them generously with a glaze. To make a sugar glaze, gently heat the sugar and water in a saucepan, stirring until the sugar has dissolved.

You will be able to just rip the buns away from the whole bake. If you want to be decadent make a little lemon icing and pipe a zig-zag pattern over the top for that extra dash of sweetness – delicious! See the recipe for this icing in the recipe for Danish Pastries on page 107.

Cinnamon Rolls

The recipe and method are exactly the same as for Chelsea Buns, but instead of spreading a mix of butter, dried fruit and sugar over the dough, spread it with a mix of butter, sugar and cinnamon (see the quantities on page 66).

150g (5oz) butter
125g (4½oz) soft dark brown sugar
6g (1 tbsp) ground cinnamon.

Beat the three ingredients together to a smooth paste. Don't be tempted to melt the butter as it will run everywhere – rely on elbow grease.

Spread over the dough and bake as per Chelsea Buns on page 66.

Doughnuts

The history of the doughnut is disputed, but one thing is certain: virtually every nationality has its own version of this delicious deep-fried bread. They are worryingly easy to make and taste divine – especially filled with a tart cherry jam.

2.5g (½ tsp) salt
225g (8oz) strong white bread flour
50g (2oz) butter
50g (2oz) caster sugar
7g (2¼ tsp) fast-action dried yeast or
    15g (½oz) fresh yeast

225ml (8 fl oz) tepid milk
1 egg, beaten
Jam, for filling (optional)
Fat for deep-frying
Caster sugar and ground cinnamon
    for coating

If using fresh yeast mix it with some of the milk and put aside for 20 minutes until frothy. Sift the salt, flour and sugar into a bowl and rub in the fat. If using fast-action yeast mix it in now or add the frothing fresh yeast mix. Mix in the remaining wet ingredients – the milk and the beaten egg – and mix to a soft dough. Knead on an unfloured board for 10 minutes.

Shape the dough into rounds – this mixture will make about 6–8 doughnuts. If you want to add jam, flatten out your round on a board, put no more than half a teaspoon of jam in the centre, then pinch the edges together and tuck them into the round and reshape into a ball. If you don't do this carefully, the doughnuts will separate as they rise, exposing the jam filling.

For doughnuts without jam, simply make a hole in the centre of the dough with a wooden spoon and spin it around on this, or on your finger, until the hole is bigger and smoother. They cook more efficiently this way as the heat gets right into the centre.

Put the doughnuts on a tray, then place the tray inside a big plastic bag and leave to prove for an hour, or a little longer if they haven't risen much, until doubled in size.

If you are using a deep-fat fryer, heat the fat to 175–180°C (350°F), or if you are just using a pan, heat until it will quickly brown a 2.5cm (1in) piece of bread. Fry the doughnuts for 3–4 minutes on each side – you can usually do a few at a time. They will turn a deep golden brown very quickly, but don't be tempted to think this means they are cooked. There is nothing worse than a doughnut with a soggy, doughy middle!

When they are cooked, drain on kitchen towels and then toss in caster sugar. If you don't use jam, try tossing them in a sugar and cinnamon mix to add some extra flavour. They are best eaten fresh – but keeping them is the problem; it's hard not to OD!

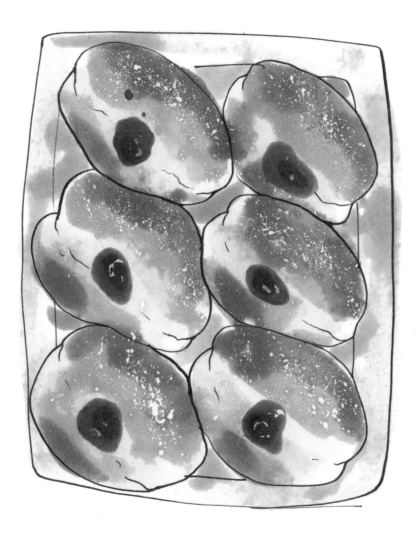

Regional Breads

Bara Brith

I grew up eating this delicious fruity Welsh bread. To serve, cut it into thin slices and butter!

5g (1 tsp) salt

450g (1lb) strong white bread flour or wholemeal flour – depending on preference

7g (1½ tsp) fast-action dried yeast or 15g (½oz) fresh yeast

75g (2½oz) butter

50g (2oz) brown sugar

6g(1 tbsp) mixed spice

225 ml (8 fl oz) strong black tea

1 egg, beaten

300g (10½oz) dried fruit (you can mix currants, sultanas, raisins and candied peel or go contemporary and add cranberries or dates to the mix)

SUGAR GLAZE

15g (1 tbsp) sugar

15ml (1 tbsp) water

Put all the dry ingredients in a bowl, except the sugar, spice and dried fruit. Rub in the butter until the mixture resembles breadcrumbs, then add the sugar and spice, and mix well. Cool the tea until it is tepid and add with the beaten egg to the mix. Use a spoon to bring the ingredients together, then go in with your hands.

When the dough forms a sticky ball, put it on a board and knead for 10 minutes. It will stay sticky for a while, but don't worry about this – just keep kneading and after 10 minutes you should have a much neater dough, though still sticky, and it will smell wonderfully spicy.

Pop this into a bowl, cover with a plastic bag and leave to prove for an hour, by which time the dough will have doubled in size.

Knock the dough back gently and add the fruit gradually, until it is all incorporated into the dough. Shape, then put into a lightly greased

1kg (2lb) loaf tin and cover with a plastic bag or cling film. Put on one side to rise for around 40 minutes.

Pre-heat the oven to 200°C (400°F), gas mark 6.

Remove the plastic and then pop the loaf into the oven for 20 minutes, then cover the top with foil, to stop the fruit burning, and bake for a further 20–25 minutes.

Put the loaf on a wire rack to cool. Make a sugar glaze by gently heating the sugar and water in a saucepan, stirring until the sugar has dissolved. Leave to cool a little, then brush over the top of the loaf. Alternatively, put a little jam or jelly preserve into a saucepan and heat gently until it is runny, then brush over the top of your loaf.

The Bara Brith is delicious eaten when still slightly warm, sliced and buttered.

Cornish Saffron Buns

This recipe comes from Jo Burgess at the National Trust's Tintagel Old Post Office. Legend has it that the Phoenicians landed in Cornwall and exchanged saffron for tin. Saffron comes from the stigma of *Crocus sativus*, as the name suggests, a member of the crocus family. It is expensive, partly because it takes 250,000 stigmas to make half a kilogram of dried saffron! In this recipe, the saffron needs to soak for up to 12 hours to allow the flavour to develop fully, so try to remember to do this well in advance of making these delicious, traditional buns. However, not everyone likes the flavour of saffron, so feel free to soak the stigma for a shorter time – the buns will still have a glorious colour. I like to add some mixed spice to this recipe; it gives the buns an extra zing.

5g (1 tsp) salt
¼–½ tsp saffron strands
300ml (½ pint) hand-hot milk
450g (1lb) strong white bread flour
7g (2¼ tsp) fast-action dried yeast or

15g (½oz) fresh yeast
150g (5oz) unsalted butter
50g (2oz) Muscovado sugar
100g (3½oz) dried fruit

Put the saffron strands in the gently warmed milk and stir well. Cover and then leave to infuse overnight, or at the very least for an hour.

Put the flour, salt and fast-action yeast into a large mixing bowl. Dice the butter and rub it in until the mixture resembles fine breadcrumbs. Stir in the sugar.

Gently warm the saffron milk until it is lukewarm and add to the other ingredients. Mix into a dough, then turn out onto a board and knead for 10 minutes. It starts off very sticky but gradually works into a deliciously smooth and elastic dough.

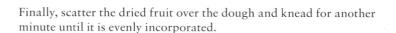

Finally, scatter the dried fruit over the dough and knead for another minute until it is evenly incorporated.

Cut and shape into approximately 12 small rounds and place them on a baking sheet. Cover with a plastic bag and leave to rise until they have doubled in size – these buns have just the one rise.

Pre-heat the oven to 180°C (350°F), gas mark 4. Bake the buns for 15–20 minutes.

Turn out onto a wire rack to cool.

Barmbrack

This is an Irish fruit loaf, which is usually eaten sliced, toasted and buttered. However, as far as my family are concerned, it's just as good eaten neat as a slice of fruit cake. Traditionally eaten at Halloween, it was baked with a coin and a ring in it; if you had the coin in your slice you'd be rich, whereas if you got the ring, you'd be married within a year. Originally it would have used fermented ale, yeast or barm, but this is my mother's recipe and she favoured tea and shop-bought yeast. It is not unheard of in our household for 50ml (2 fl oz) of the liquid to be substituted with a little Irish whiskey.

2.5g (½ tsp) salt

7g (2¼ tsp) fast-action dried yeast or
    15g (½ oz) fresh yeast

100g (3½ oz) caster sugar

300ml (½ pint) tea (perhaps
    substitute whiskey for a measure or
    two of the water)

450g (1lb) strong white bread flour

1g (½ tsp) mixed spice

2 eggs

75g (2½ oz) butter

100g (3½ oz) sultanas

100g (3½ oz) currants

100g (3½ oz) raisins

25g (1oz) mixed peel

GLAZE

15ml (1 tbsp) water

20g (1 tbsp) granulated sugar

If you are using fresh yeast, blend it with 1 level teaspoon of the sugar and the tepid water or tea. If you are using fast-action dried yeast, incorporate it with the dry ingredients.

Sift the flour, spice and salt into a bowl. Add the yeast mixture and mix well – the easiest way to do this is to get stuck in with your hands and give it a light knead to make sure all the ingredients are thoroughly incorporated.

Cover with a plastic bag and leave to rise in a warm place for an hour.

Then, when the dough has risen, beat the eggs, heat the butter gently (just enough to melt it) and add them to the dough along with the rest of the sugar and the dried fruit and mixed peel. This is a really sloppy mix and, again, you'll have to use your hands to bring all the ingredients together and ensure they are evenly incorporated. It will feel more like a Christmas cake mix than a dough.

Grease a 20cm (8in) cake tin. Place the dough in the tin, cover with a plastic bag and leave in a warm place for about an hour until it has doubled in size.

Pre-heat the oven to 200°C (400°F), gas mark 6 and bake for about an hour. If it looks as though the top of the barmbrack is beginning to catch at the edges, cover it with some baking parchment to help protect it.

While it is cooking, prepare the glaze. Put the sugar and water in a pan and heat gently until the sugar has dissolved. You can use melted jam if you prefer – melted spiced crab apple jelly is heavenly.

When the loaf is cooked, remove from the oven and brush with the glaze before popping it back into the oven for a minute or two. Remove and cool on a wire rack.

Lardy Cake

Lardy Cake comes from Wiltshire and can be served as a cake or as a pudding. Don't let the addition of the lard discourage you; this is heaven on earth, and quite different in flavour and texture to other fruit breads.

10g (2 tsp) salt
7g (2¼ tsp) fast-action dried yeast or
  15g (½oz) fresh yeast
300ml (½ pint) tepid water
450g (1lb) strong white bread flour
15ml (1 tbsp) vegetable oil

50g (2oz) butter
100g (3½oz) caster sugar
2g (1 tsp) mixed spice
75g (2½oz) sultanas
50g (2oz) lard

Grease a 25 x 20cm (10 x 8in) roasting tin. Mix the fresh yeast with the water. Sift the flour and salt into a basin, stir in the yeast mixture and oil, and mix to a soft dough. Beat until the mixture is smooth, then cover with cling film and leave to rise until the mixture has approximately doubled in size.

Turn the dough onto a lightly floured surface and knead for 5–10 minutes.

Roll out into a rectangle about 6mm (¼in) thick. Dot small pieces of the butter across two-thirds of the surface and sprinkle with 3 tablespoons of the sugar. Then sprinkle with half the spice and dried fruit. Fold the dough over into thirds and roll it, then fold again into thirds and re-roll. Repeat this process until the butter is incorporated into the dough.

Roll out into a rectangle again and repeat the process, this time using the lard cut into small pieces, 3 tablespoons of sugar and the remaining fruit and spice. Repeat the folding and rolling process.

Roll the dough out until it's approximately the size of the tin, then place it inside the greased tin and press it down until it fits into the corners. Cover with cling film and leave in a warm place until it has doubled in size.

Pre-heat the oven to 220°C (425°F), gas mark 7.

Sprinkle the dough with a little caster sugar and mark the top with crosses using a knife.

Bake for about 30 minutes. Cool on a wire rack. Serve sliced, either plain, or buttered.

Sally Lunn

It's hard to ascertain the truth behind the legend of the Sally Lunn bun. According to legend, Sally Lunn was a French Huguenot who arrived in Britain in 1680. She worked in a bakery in Bath and is reputed to have introduced the locals to her own form of French breakfast cake. The Sally Lunn Eating House is one of the oldest buildings in Bath but was acquired and turned into its present form only in 1925. Eliza Acton maintains that the origins are from the French *solimemne*.

5g (1 tsp) salt
50g (2oz) butter
200ml (7 fl oz) milk
4g (1 tsp) caster sugar
7g (2¼ tsp) fast-action dried yeast or
    15g (½oz) fresh yeast
2 eggs, beaten

450g (1lb) strong white bread flour
Glaze
30ml (2 tbsp) water
25g (2 tbsp) sugar
Optional
170g (6oz) mixed dried fruit

Melt the butter gently in a pan, remove from the heat and add the milk and sugar, mix well. Add the fresh yeast and the beaten eggs and mix again.

Sift the flour and salt together, then add the milk and yeast mixture. If you wish to use dried fruit, add it now. Mix well and knead lightly.

Grease two 13cm (5in) cake tins. Divide the dough into two pieces, then shape into rounds. Put them into the tins and cover with a plastic bag.

Put in a warm place and leave to rise for about 45 minutes or until the dough rises up well.

Pre-heat the oven to 230°C (450°F), gas mark 8. Bake for 15–20 minutes

While your Sally Lunn buns are baking, heat the sugar and water together to make your glaze.

When the buns are cooked, place them on a wire tray to cool and brush them over with the glaze while still warm.

A Sally Lunn is traditionally served split in half and either buttered or filled with whipped cream!

Hot-Cross Buns

Traditionally consumed on Good Friday, but delicious all year round, you don't need to add the pastry crosses except at Easter. Hot-cross buns became immensely popular in Tudor times, as you were only permitted to eat such spiced bread on special occasions, such as Easter, Christmas and at funerals, after a decree in 1592. The cross on the buns used to be simply made with a knife, which you can do, too, if you can't be bothered to make the paste for the cross.

5g (1 tsp) salt
450g (1lb) strong white bread flour
12g (2½ tsp) fast-action dried yeast
  or 25g (1oz) fresh yeast
50g (2oz) caster sugar
2g (1 tsp) mixed spice
1g (½ tsp) ground cinnamon
1g (½ tsp) ground nutmeg
50g (2oz) butter, melted and cooled
1 egg, beaten
150ml (5 fl oz) warm milk

60ml (4 tbsp) warm water
100g (3½oz) dried fruit (mix of
  raisins, sultanas and currants)
25g (1oz) chopped mixed peel
FOR THE CROSSES
50g (2oz) plain white flour
100ml (3½ fl oz) water
GLAZE
30ml (2 tbsp) milk
30ml (2 tbsp) water
45g (1½oz) caster sugar

If using fresh yeast, blend it with the milk and water and add 100g (3½oz) flour. Put aside for 15–20 minutes, until frothy.

Put the salt, the flour, sugar and spices into a bowl. Add the cooled melted butter, the beaten egg, yeast mixture and fruit, and bring together into a dough. Knead for about 10 minutes.

Put in a bowl and cover with a plastic bag and leave somewhere warm until doubled in size (1–2 hours).

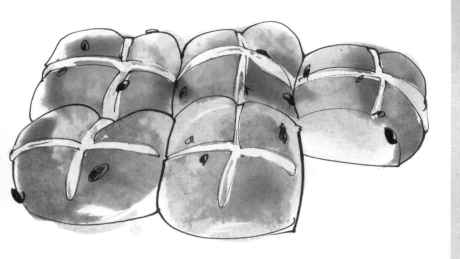

Place the dough on a wooden board and knock back gently. This mixture should make about 12 buns, so divide the dough, shape into round buns, put on a baking sheet and cover with a plastic bag. Leave in a warm place until doubled in size.

Pre-heat the oven to 200°C (400°F), gas mark 6

If you want to put crosses on the top, prepare the flour and water mix while your buns are proving. Whisk the flour and water together and pop it into a piping bag – if you have one – or if you're disorganised like me, chances are you'll use a small plastic bag with a tiny hole snipped in the corner.

Make crosses with a knife in the top of each bun and pipe your flour and water paste into this.

Bake in the oven for 15–20 minutes, until golden.

While the buns are cooking, gently heat the milk, water and caster sugar gently together to make your glaze.

As soon as the buns come out of the oven, brush the tops a couple of times with the sugar glaze.

Bath Buns

These were created in the eighteenth century. The rich and famous indulged in a Bath Bun after taking the waters.

5g (1 tsp) salt
450g (1lb) strong white bread flour
12g (4 tsp) fast-action dried yeast or
    25g (1oz) fresh yeast
150ml (¼ pint) tepid milk
60ml (4 tbsp) tepid water
50g (2oz) caster sugar

2 eggs, beaten
50g (2oz) butter, melted and cooled
170g (6oz) sultanas
25g (1oz) mixed peel
TOPPING
Beaten egg
Caster sugar

Grease two baking sheets. Mix the fresh yeast, milk and water and 100g (3½oz) of the flour together and leave in a warm place for 20 minutes, until the mixture is frothy.

Sift the remaining flour and salt into a bowl and add the sugar. Then stir in the eggs, butter, yeast mixture, sultanas and peel, and mix to a soft wet dough. Turn onto a lightly floured board and knead for 5–10 minutes until smooth.

Put the dough into a bowl and cover with plastic. Leave to rise in a warm place until doubled in size (1–2 hours). Give the mix a gentle stir, then place spoonfuls of the mixture onto the baking sheets and cover with plastic bags, ensuring the plastic isn't touching the dough. Leave to rise in a warm place until doubled in size. When the buns have risen, brush with egg and sprinkle with sugar.

Pre-heat the oven to 190°C (375°F), gas mark 5.

Bake for about 15 minutes, until a light golden brown. Cool on a wire rack, then split and serve buttered.

Cornish Splits

This recipe comes from Jo Burgess at Tintagel Old Post Office and makes a deliciously soft roll.

5g (1 tsp) salt
50g (2oz) butter
300ml (½ pint) milk
450g (1lb) strong white bread flour
7g (2¼ tsp) fast-action dried yeast or

15g (½oz) fresh yeast
15g (1 tbsp) caster sugar
TOPPING
Butter
Icing sugar

Melt the butter and put on one side to cool. Warm the milk to blood temperature – hand hot. Mix the flour, salt, sugar and yeast together in a large bowl. Add the melted butter and warm milk, and mix to a soft dough.

Knead on a lightly floured board for 10 minutes – this is a sticky dough but just keep working at it like an enthusiastic six-year-old and you'll feel it get smoother and more cohesive.

Pop into an oiled bowl and cover with a plastic bag until doubled in size, approximately an hour.

Put on a lightly floured board and knock back gently for a few minutes. This mix will give you around nine splits, so divide the dough evenly and shape into rounds. Pop them onto a greased and lightly floured baking tray.

Cover with a plastic bag and leave to prove for half an hour until well risen.

Pre-heat the oven to 220°C (430°F), gas mark 8. Bake for 15 minutes.

Split them as soon as they come out of the oven – rub a hint of butter over the tops – and cover with a linen cloth if you don't want them to develop a crust. Finish off with a dusting of icing sugar.

These rolls are absolutely delicious – the Cornish eat them hot, buttered and served with clotted cream and jam. They are a lighter version of scones!

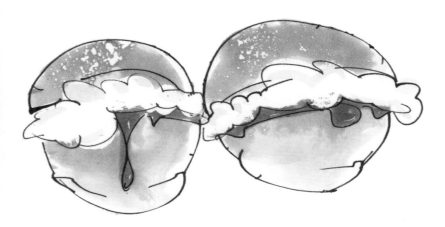

Breads from Around the World

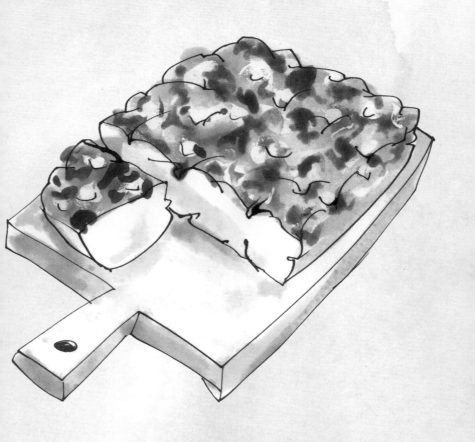

Bread in the French Fashion

This recipe comes from the National Trust's Moseley Old Hall, where King Charles I hid after the Battle of Worcester in 1651. Bakers maintain that French bread is very hard to make without French flour, French water and a French baker's oven. This recipe is an old English attempt to reproduce a French loaf.

5g (1 tsp) salt
12g (4 tsp) fast-action dried yeast or
  25g (1oz) fresh yeast
2g (½ tsp) sugar
300ml (½ pint) tepid milk

1 egg, beaten
450g (1lb) strong white bread flour
75g (2½oz) butter
Milk or beaten egg for brushing

Cream the fresh yeast with the sugar. Warm the milk gently, add the beaten egg and pour about half of this into the yeast and stir.

Put the flour into a bowl, cut the butter into small pieces and rub into the flour. Add the yeast mixture and the rest of the egg and milk mixture and mix to a sticky dough.

Knead for about 8–10 minutes and then transfer the dough to a warm, oiled bowl. Cover with a plastic bag and leave in a warm place until the dough has doubled in size.

Knock the dough back gently and shape to fit a greased and floured 450g (1lb) tin.

Allow the dough to rise for about an hour until it has risen to fill three-quarters of the tin.

Pre-heat the oven to 230°C (450°F), gas mark 8.

When the loaf has proved, brush the loaf with milk or an egg wash
and put it into the oven for around 25 minutes. Cool on a wire rack
before cutting.

Ciabatta

You need to make your starter at least 12 hours before you make your loaf, so make sure that you take this into account when making the ciabatta.

FOR THE STARTER:
115g (4oz) very strong white flour
2.5g (¾ tsp) fast-action dried yeast or
   7g (¼oz) fresh yeast
4g (1 tsp sugar)
150ml (¼ pint) tepid water

FOR THE LOAF:
5g (1 tsp) salt
350g (12oz) strong white bread flour
5g (1¾ tsp) fast-action dried yeast or
   10g (⅓oz) fresh yeast
60ml (4 tbsp) extra virgin olive oil
200ml (7 fl oz) tepid water

Put all the ingredients for the starter into a bowl and mix to a smooth batter. Cover the bowl and put on one side for at least 12 hours before making the bread.

When your starter is ready, put the flour, yeast and salt into a large bowl (this mix will grow, so you need to be able to accommodate it), mix together, then add the starter dough, the olive oil and a little of the water. Mix together until all the ingredients are incorporated – it may be a little lumpy. Then, little by little, mix in the remaining water. There is much talk at this point of turning on the mixer, but I don't have one and feel very strongly that no one should assume we all do. So, if you have a mixer, wham it on until the mix is very smooth and elastic. If, like me, you use your hands, get stuck in to the mixing bowl. I love making ciabatta; it is such a sensual experience, the mix is very sticky, and, as you work it, it becomes smoother and stretchier.

Cover with a plastic bag and put on one side for 2 hours, by which time the loaf should have grown to around three times its original size.

Grease and lightly flour a baking sheet.

Gently tip the dough onto a floured board – you want to retain as much air as possible – and shape the loaf into an oblong, tucking in the ends underneath.

Dust the loaf with flour, put aside and leave to prove, uncovered, for 45 minutes. Pre-heat the oven to 220°C (425°F), gas mark 7.

Gently ease the dough onto the prepared baking sheet and bake for 15–20 minutes. When it is cooked, pop it onto a wire tray to cool.

Wild Garlic Focaccia

This recipe comes courtesy of Hattie Ells, who runs the cafe at the
National Trust's Glendurgan Garden in the Cornish north Helford
countryside. Hattie uses the leaves of *Allium Ursinum*, otherwise
known as ramsoms, or wild garlic, which grow abundantly in
the nearby woods in spring, as well as rosemary. You can make it
without the wild garlic out of season and it's just as delicious.

5g (1 tsp) salt
350g (12oz) strong white bread flour
7g (2¼ tsp) fast-action dried yeast or
    15g (½oz) fresh yeast
60ml (4 tbsp) olive oil
200ml (7 fl oz) water

A good handful of fresh rosemary
    leaves, chopped
Approximately 30g (1oz) wild garlic,
    freshly picked and finely chopped
Olive oil for drizzling
Fine sea salt

Place the salt, flour, fast-action yeast, 3 tablespoons of the olive oil
and the water in a mixing bowl. Stir gently to form a dough and then
knead for 10 minutes.

Add the rosemary and chopped wild garlic, and knead until the herbs
are incorporated evenly throughout the dough.

Pour the last tablespoon of olive oil into a bowl, pop the dough into it
and roll it over, so that it is coated in oil. Cover the bowl with a plastic
bag and leave the dough to rise until doubled in size – approximately
1–1½ hours.

Turn the dough out onto a lightly floured board, and shape it into
a flattened circle. Pop it onto a baking sheet and then cover with a
plastic bag for another hour.

Pre-heat the oven to 220°C (425°F), gas mark 8.

Lightly press the top of the dough with your finger to make little dimples – a regular pattern looks good. Drizzle with olive oil and sprinkle with sea salt.

Bake in the pre-heated oven for about 15 minutes, until the top is a lovely appetising golden brown.

This bread is equally delicious served hot or cold – and it is lovely served with some good-quality olive oil and balsamic vinegar for dipping.

Pizza Dough

This mix makes a good-sized pizza for two people to share.

5g (1 tsp) salt
7g (2¼ tsp) fast-action dried yeast or
   15g (½oz) fresh yeast
4g (1 tsp) sugar

150ml (¼ pint) water
225g (8oz) strong white bread flour
75ml (5 tbsp) olive oil

If you are using fresh yeast, dissolve the yeast and sugar in some of the water and set aside to ferment for 10–15 minutes.

Sieve the flour and salt into a bowl. If you are using fast-action yeast, add it to the dry ingredients. Pour in the yeast mixture, the oil and the rest of the water, and mix well.

Knead the dough for 10 minutes, then put it in a bowl, cover with a plastic bag and set aside to rise.

Knock back lightly. Now this is the fun bit: put the dough onto a lightly floured board, lightly flour your hands and flatten it a little. Spin it around in your hands allowing its own weight to stretch it until you have a circle about 25cm (10in) in diameter. It's harder to do than the professionals make it look, but don't worry too much – you'll get better with practice and it'll taste great whatever it looks like.

Place it on a lightly greased and floured baking tray – or a baking stone or pizza stone if you have one.

Pre-heat the oven to as hot as it will go.

Place whatever topping you want on the top of the dough and bake for about 10–15 minutes until golden brown.

Pitta Bread

This basic bread has been used for centuries in parts of the Mediterranean and the Middle East and is now deservedly popular the world over. It is deliciously easy to make.

5g (1 tsp) salt
350g (12oz) strong white or
wholemeal bread flour

5g (1 ¾ tsp) fast-action dried yeast or
12g (½ oz) fresh yeast
225ml (8 fl oz) water

If you are using fast-action yeast, put all the ingredients in a bowl and mix together before kneading for 10 minutes on a board. If you are using fresh yeast, mix it with a little of the water and leave in a warm place for 10–15 minutes. Add this to the rest of the water when you are ready to combine it with the dry ingredients. Pour the water into the dry ingredients, mix together and knead for 10 minutes on a board.

Pop the kneaded dough into a bowl, cover with a plastic bag and leave to rest for 15 minutes.

Knead briefly, then divide the dough into 4–6 pieces, depending on how big you like your pitta, and roll into balls.

Leave the balls to rest for 5 minutes under a linen cloth.

Take each piece and roll out into a circle, somewhere around 6mm (¼in) thick. Place on a lightly floured baking sheet, cover with a linen cloth and leave for 25 minutes.

Pre-heat the oven to 220°C (425°F), gas mark 7.

Bake the pitta breads for about 8 minutes, and split them as soon as they come out of the oven. Eat while warm or toast them to reheat.

Danish Pastries

Despite their name, Danish pastries actually hailed originally from Vienna. They are fiendishly fiddly to make, the method being broadly similar to croissant dough, and the calories are positively terrifying, but they're really good! And you can have fun creating all manner of fillings to suit you, and your family's taste preferences. Perhaps make some confectioner's custard, topped with a piece of stewed or even canned fruit – a Danish is the one pastry where canned fruit seems to shine, especially apricots. Just make sure that each piece of fruit is well drained – you don't want the proverbial soggy bottom! Chez Eastoe the preference is strictly traditional, and the fillings listed below are our favourites. To make your life easier, you can make the dough the evening before and pop it into the fridge overnight. Then all you have to do the following morning is the shaping and final proving and you'll have delicious Danish pastries ready for elevenses. Please read this recipe all the way through before you start making the pastries; it's very important that you understand the timings and process.

5g (1 tsp) salt

250g (9oz) butter

12g (4 tsp) fast-action dried yeast or
   25g (1oz) fresh yeast

150ml (¼ pint) tepid milk

450g (1lb) plain white flour

30g (2 tbsp) sugar

2½ eggs, beaten

GLAZE

Beaten egg

The first thing to do is to attempt to get your butter more the shape of the dough you will ultimately place it in – longer and thinner than the pat in front of you. Take two sheets of baking paper – approximately 25cm (10in) square. Put one sheet on the table, place the butter in the middle of it, then cover with the other sheet. Take a rolling pin and gently roll the butter out – you want a strip of around 20 x 13cm (8 x

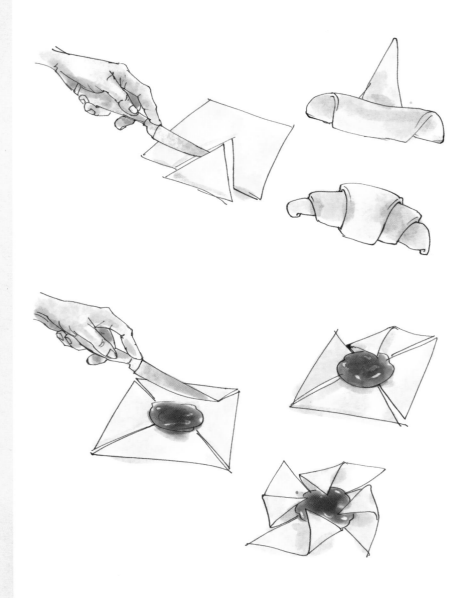

5in), so don't roll it out to fit the paper. Leave the butter in the paper and pop it into the fridge to chill.

If you are using fresh yeast, mix it into the tepid milk and leave it for 15 minutes, until it is getting a little frothy. Sift the salt and flour into a bowl, then add the sugar. If you are using fast-action yeast, add it now and mix the ingredients together. Add the milk and eggs and work to a soft dough. Turn the dough out onto a board and knead for 10 minutes until smooth. Pop it back into the bowl, cover and leave it to rest in the fridge for 10 minutes.

On a lightly floured work surface, roll the dough out until it is at least three times as long as the piece of butter, and a little wider. Place the butter in the centre of the dough, and fold the long sides of the dough over the butter so that there is a good overlap. Press down along the join to seal the seam and do the same thing at each end – you are aiming to contain the butter.

Roll the dough out into a long rectangle that is three times as long as it is wide, ideally up to about 45cm (18in) in length. Fold the top third down and the bottom third up. Place in a bowl, cover and leave to rest for 10 minutes. Take it out of the bowl and repeat this process twice more. When you have done this, cover it again and leave it to rest for 30 minutes. Pre-heat the oven to 220°C (425°F), gas mark 7.

Now for the fun part: it is time to select what shape of Danish pastry you want to make – crescents, imperial stars, cushions or pinwheels (all the techniques are described on page 34). Roll out the dough to the prescribed thickness, cutting and popping your filling of choice in place (see pages 106–107).

When you have shaped your dough, leave it to prove for 30 minutes, then brush with some beaten egg and bake in the pre-heated oven for about 15 minutes until the pastries have turned a lovely pale gold colour. While they are still hot, put your icing (see page 107) into a piping bag and pipe zig-zag shapes across them and possibly sprinkle a few chopped or flaked almonds over the top.

Cinnamon Butter Filling

My family adore this filling in pinwheel Danish pastries.

50g (2oz) butter, softened
50g (2oz) caster sugar
4g (2 tsp) ground cinnamon

Cream the butter and sugar together until smooth, then add the cinnamon and beat into the mix. Spread this over the dough and roll it up for delicious breakfast Danish pastries.

Almond Paste Filling

15g (½oz) butter
75g (2½oz) caster sugar

75g (2½oz) ground almonds
1 egg, beaten

Cream the butter and sugar together until smooth, add the ground almonds and mix well. Put the beaten egg in a jug and add a little at a time to the mix – you are aiming to achieve a lovely soft, spreading consistency. This is lovely in crescent shaped Danish pastries – rather like an almond croissant!

Crème Pâtissière

Crème pâtissière works best in shapes such as cushions and imperial stars where the custard is slightly contained. Top the custard with a fruit of your choice, I am a sucker for canned apricot halves, shame on me, or raspberries, but let your imagination run riot, and finish off with some flaked almonds and a zig-zag flourish of lemon icing.

4 egg yolks
50g (2oz) caster sugar
1 vanilla pod or a few drops of vanilla essence

25g (1oz) plain flour
4g (2 tsp) cornflour
280ml (10 fl oz) milk

Put the egg yolks into a bowl, add the sugar and the vanilla (just the seeds from the inside if using a pod) and beat well, then whisk in both flours. Heat the milk gently until close to boiling, then remove from the heat. Add some of the milk to the egg mixture and beat well, then add this mix to the rest of the milk in the saucepan and give it a good stir. Put the pan back onto a gentle heat and stir until the mixture is simmering and thickening. Don't be tempted to leave it – you need to keep stirring. Remove from the heat.

Icing

50g (2oz) icing sugar

7.5ml (1 ½ tsp) lemon juice

To make the icing, mix the icing sugar and lemon juice together until smooth and drizzle, dribble or pipe it over the pastries.

Baguette

While the precise ancestry of the baguette is a matter for debate, it is generally agreed that it hit the market big time in the 1920s. Steam is integral to the production of a perfect baguette, but steam ovens were not introduced until the nineteenth century. Its surge in popularity had more to do with a set of government restrictions, introduced in the 1920s, that banned bakers from working between the hours of 10pm and 4am. As baguettes could be prepared and baked more rapidly than traditional breads, they enabled bakers to supply bread from first thing in the morning. There is nothing like a French baguette, so don't expect too much from this recipe.

5g (1 tsp) salt
7g (2¼ tsp) fast-action dried yeast or
   15g (½oz) fresh yeast
300ml (½ pint) tepid water

4g (1 tsp) caster sugar350g (12 oz)
   strong white bread flour
125g (4½oz) French bread flour (or
   strong white bread flour)

If you are using fresh yeast, put it in a bowl with a little of the tepid water and the sugar, and mix to a smooth blend. Put on one side for 15–20 minutes, until frothy. When the yeast mix is ready add it along with the rest of the water as per the instructions below.

Mix all the dry ingredients in a bowl, add the yeast and water and mix together to form a soft dough. Turn this onto a board and knead for at least 10 minutes – the dough will be soft, pliable and quite wet. Oil a bowl and put the dough into it, cover with a plastic bag or shower cap and then leave to rise until doubled in size, which will take about an hour.

Grease a large baking sheet and flour it lightly.

The dough will make two baguettes – make sure you don't make them so long that they won't fit into your oven!

Gently put the dough onto a clean board and divide into two pieces. You should be very gentle with it as you want to keep as much air in it as you possibly can, so don't knock it back.

Flatten each piece of dough out gently into a long and thin rectangle – you might want to use a light rolling pin to help you. Roll the dough up tightly into a long sausage and then pinch the seams together. Place the baguettes on the floured baking sheet with the seam side downwards. Cover with a large plastic bag and leave to prove for about an hour.

Pre-heat the oven to 220°C (425F°), gas mark 7.

Boil a kettle of water and get a roasting tin ready – you want to pop this into the oven on a low shelf moments before putting the baguettes into the oven.

Uncover the baguettes, dust them with flour and make 3 or 4 diagonal slashes along the length with a sharp knife.

Pop into the oven and bake for 20 minutes, until golden brown. Cool on a wire tray – if you can wait – and eat very fresh as this bread does not keep well!

Gluten-Free Loaf

Given the traditional nature of the recipes in this book this is the only one that offers a gluten-free option. Nevertheless, all enthusiastic bread makers should have at least one good gluten-free recipe at their disposal as gluten intolerance and coeliac disease are becoming increasingly common. Unfortunately, you cannot simply substitute gluten-free flour for bread flour in any given recipe; it behaves quite differently and, with no gluten structure to develop, no kneading is required. Eggs are often incorporated into the recipe as they are good leavening agents, and olive oil helps to produce a more flavoursome bread.

Gluten-free flour is readily available in most supermarkets and on the internet.

Please be sure to take the greatest care when you are baking gluten-free bread to avoid any potential cross-contamination with wheat flour via cooking utensils and work surfaces.

5g (1 tsp) salt
450g (1lb) gluten-free flour
30g (2½ tbsp) caster sugar
10g (2 tsp) fast-action dried yeast

330ml (11 fl oz) milk
2 eggs, beaten
5ml (1 tsp) wine or cider vinegar
105ml (7 tbsp) olive oil

Oil a 1kg (2lb) loaf tin. Put all the dry ingredients in a bowl and mix together thoroughly.

Warm the milk a little, add to the beaten eggs and then add the vinegar and beat well.

Stir the milk, eggs and vinegar mixture into the dry ingredients – you can use a fork to bring everything together, but don't expect to produce a dough. What you will get is something that will ultimately resemble a cake mixture. Add the oil, a tablespoonful at a time, and keep working away with your fork until the mixture is all incorporated. Spoon into the tin and cover with a shower cap or plastic bag. Put in a warm place to almost double in size – this will take around an hour.

Pre-heat the oven to 220°C (425°F), gas mark 7.

Boil a kettle, pour the water into a roasting tin and put it into the oven on a low shelf a few minutes before the mixture goes in. The steam will help to produce a better loaf.

Place the loaf tin on the shelf above the roasting tin for around 40 minutes, but keep an eye out for the last 5 minutes as it may need a little more or less baking time. A baking thermometer will be particularly useful in letting you know that the loaf is cooked to the centre. If it reaches 98°C (208°F) it's done. Gluten-free bread goes dry very quickly – but the leftovers make a fabulous bread and butter pudding.

Sourdough

Achingly fashionable, sourdough has its own distinctive flavour and may well be the one bread you wish to make immediately. Restrain the impulse. Despite what celebrity chefs maintain, making sourdough bread is not a doddle. Most people, myself included, usually have many attempts before they get it right. I don't want a sourdough catastrophe to discourage you from bread making per se, so please, please, please become confident in the art of bread making before you try your hand at sourdough.

For me the chief difficulty is organisational: sourdough, like marriage and raising children, demands commitment and routine. Firstly you have to create and feed your starter – with precise quantities of flour and water – at regular intervals. You also have to remove the excess starter daily, which, in my mind, is a remarkably wasteful but essential part of the process. When, after around eight days, your starter is getting suitably lively, neither too strong in flavour, nor too weak to do the job, you can set about making your bread.

Producing a 'sponge' – simply a more concentrated mix of flour and water combined with a good dollop of starter – is the next stage and this has to 'rest' for around 8–12 hours.

The next step is to add the rest of the ingredients required to the starter and knead the dough, but this is not the end of the process! The dough has to be tweaked and cosseted at regular intervals over the next three hours – I've had sick dogs that were less demanding – and then proved for 2–4 hours. Finally, it is ready for baking in a good steamy oven.

I am really and truly not trying to put you off sourdough, more to mentally prepare you for the effort required. I believe that once you get into a rhythm, making sourdough becomes a natural process, but it does require a level of commitment that is quite difficult for anyone who works nine to five.

Please give sourdough your best shot; these recipes work if you follow them faithfully. Perhaps take heart from the knowledge that my first seven attempts failed, a disheartening period that my nearest and dearest dubbed 'the sourdough years'.

Sourdough Bread

Allow eight days before you plan to make your bread to create your starter. Once it is underway you can keep it going indefinitely and pop it to sleep in the fridge for a week before getting it going again when required. The sponge will require 12 hours – it's good to do this before you go to bed on a Friday or Saturday night, then you have the next day to repeatedly deflate and shape the dough over three hours before proving the dough for 2–4 hours. Baking is the easy bit!

Sourdough Starter:

DAY ONE
75g (2½oz) wholemeal or rye flour
125ml (4½ fl oz) tepid water

Get a plastic bowl with a firm lid. Put the flour and water into the bowl and mix it together well to introduce plenty of air. I use a hand whisk for this. Then pop it into a warm place, such as an airing cupboard, for 24 hours. Make sure the container has plenty of room for more feedings because you are going to keep adding to it. Keep an eye on it – it should start to bubble within 24 hours, but it could take a little longer. It will also start to acquire a ferociously yeasty smell – one that clears my children out of the kitchen in seconds. When this happens it is ready for its first feed.

FIRST FEED: 125ml (4½ fl oz) tepid water
75g (2½oz) wholemeal flour

Add the ingredients, stir and cover and put on one side for 24 hours. The starter can now live in the kitchen – if you keep it in the airing cupboard the chances are you won't remember to feed it daily.

MAINTENANCE FEEDS:
75g (2½ oz) wholemeal flour
125ml (4½ fl oz) tepid water

Discard about half of your mix – I don't recommend using the sink as it tends to clog it up. Then add the maintenance feed, give it a good whisk and put to one side. Repeat this process daily for at least six days, by when your starter should be ready to use. It will smell pretty strong and the mix may separate, but don't worry about this. Whisk it up, chuck half away, add the new ingredients, give it another whisk and cover, leave for 24 hours, and so on...

At the end of this process you will have a lively starter. You will not use all your starter in one go; the aim is to keep it going so that you always have a starter whenever you need it. Put it into the fridge if you don't need to use it for a while, and it will, essentially, lie dormant until you need it next. It doesn't need feeding in the fridge. I don't like to leave it in the fridge for longer than a week to ten days at the most, but some people maintain it can stay there unused for ages. This hasn't worked for me, but you may have better luck. If you want to use the starter when it has been in the fridge take it out, whisk it up and give it its maintenance feed, then leave it for 24 hours to come back to life.

If you leave your starter at room temperature without discarding and feeding it, it will go mouldy and you will have to throw it away.

Making the Sponge:

This mix will make you one nice loaf; if you want to make more, just double or triple the quantities accordingly.

250g (9oz) wholemeal or strong white bread flour

300ml (½ pint) warm water
75ml (2½ fl oz) sourdough starter

Mix these ingredients together and give them a good whisk. Cover with plastic and leave somewhere warm for 8–12 hours.

Making the Bread:

As stated before, this mix will make you one nice loaf; adjust amounts accordingly to make more.

12g (2½ tsp) salt
300g (10½oz) strong white bread

flour or wholemeal flour
300ml (½ pint) water

Mix these ingredients with the refreshed sourdough starter (sponge) in a bowl. Then place on an unfloured board and knead for about 10 minutes, until the dough is soft and silky. A wholewheat flour dough may take a little longer to feel silky than a strong white flour mix. Shape the dough into a nice round, then flour the bowl and pop the dough back into it, cover with a plastic bag and allow it to rest for an hour.

Repeat this process twice more, resting for an hour each time! The dough will not rise very much, but you will feel it getting less sticky and smoother.

Now for proving the dough and this is where a proving basket comes into its own. Flour the basket very heavily – give it a good shake around and get the flour into all the nooks and crannies. Shape the dough into a lovely smooth round, flour it liberally and put it head first into the proving basket. If you don't use loads of flour the dough may stick when you try to remove it and the loaf will become a little misshapen.

Cover it with a plastic bag or a shower cap, and make sure the plastic won't touch the dough – it will stick if it does and spoil the shape of the bread.

If you don't have a proving basket, pop the shaped dough onto a floured board, support it with a floured tea towel or linen cloth and then place it inside a big plastic bag and leave it for 4–5 hours. If you need to, you can use glasses or cups to keep the plastic away from the dough – feel free. If the dough rises quickly, you can give it less proving time but sourdough generally likes a long time to prove. Either way, leave the dough to prove for 4–5 hours.

Pre-heat the oven to its maximum temperature.

Put your baking sheet or baking stone into the oven to heat up for a few minutes before the loaf goes into the oven.

Boil a kettle and get a roasting tray ready – you want the loaf to cook in a steamy oven as this will help to give you a nice crisp crust. The tray of water goes on the shelf below the loaf.

Take the tray or baking stone out of the oven – be sure to use gloves for this!

If you used a proving basket, turn the dough out onto the baking sheet gently – you don't want it to lose any air. If it falls out with a thump it will deflate a little. Your dough should have a lovely floury pattern and be a perfect round. Don't despair if it doesn't turn out perfectly, it'll still have an interesting pattern. On your next attempt use more flour on the basket and dough. Put the sheet into the oven, followed by a roasting tray full of boiling water onto the shelf below.

If you don't have a proving basket, gently transfer your dough to the baking sheet. You can spray the top lightly with water, or if you don't have a spray just splash some drops on with your fingertips.

Slash the top of the dough with a knife to make a nice pattern and quickly pop the baking sheet into the oven, followed rapidly by the roasting tray full of boiling water.

Cook the bread at the maximum temperature for 10 minutes, then turn it down to 200°C (400°F), gas mark 6. Cook for another 20–30 minutes, by which time it should have reached an internal temperature of 98°C (208°F) and be perfectly cooked. If you know your oven is a little fierce, or the loaf appears to be burning, lower the temperature accordingly.

Cool the loaf on a wire tray.

Don't be in a hurry to eat it; sourdough has a brilliant shelf life. Indeed, I prefer the flavour when it is at least 24 hours old.

GLOSSARY OF TERMS

Banneton
A banneton is a basket that is used to both support the dough during the proving process and to create a decorative finish.

Barm
A rising agent obtained in the process of brewing, widely used before the introduction of commercial yeast.

Crumb
The interior structure of bread.

Dough
A basic mixture of flour, water and yeast that requires kneading.

Dust
A light sprinkling of flour over the dough.

Extraction
The percentage of whole grain found in different flours.

Fermentation
The process whereby yeast converts sugars into carbon dioxide, which gives dough both volume and flavour.

Glaze
Brushing the surface of proved dough with sugar-syrup, egg, milk or water to produce a glossy finish.

Gluten
A combination of the proteins gliadin and glutenin that form elastic gluten chains in the kneading process, giving the dough its structure and supporting the carbon dioxide bubbles.

Griddle
A heated metal surface that is used to cook thin regional breads such as pikelets and welsh cakes.

Knead
The method of working the dough mix with your fingers, knuckles and palms to develop the gluten chains and promote elasticity.

Knock-back
The process of removing the gas from the dough after it has risen – a less violent process that it sounds.

Lame
A blade used by bakers to score dough.

Oven spring
The last rise of the dough in the heat of the oven, before it reaches a temperature that inhibits the action of the yeast.

Peel

A long-handled, thin shovel used to transfer dough and bread into and out of the oven.

Poolish

A term that is popular in America for a pre-fermented dough, as is commonly used in baguettes.

Prove

Putting the kneaded dough on one side to rise until it has doubled in size. The term is commonly used to describe the second rise.

Rise

The expansion of dough during fermentation.

Rub in

Working fat into flour by rubbing the ingredients between the thumbs and fingers, thereby creating fine crumbs.

Score

Cutting the dough across the surface immediately before it goes into the oven to aid rising.

Shaping

Forming dough into its final shape before its final proving.

Sourdough

A dough that uses fermented wild yeast to act as a rising agent via a starter.

Sponge

This is a batter-like mix of flour, water and yeast that is left to ferment for a length of time up to 24 hours, prior to combining all the ingredients for bread making. The purpose is to soften the gluten, to add flavour and to encourage the production of yeast.

Starter

A batter made from specific flours, mixed with water, generating the production of wild yeast over four or five days.

Tepid

Liquid that is body heat – 37°C (98.4°F) – the ideal temperature to activate yeast. When you put your finger into it, it should feel neither warm, nor cold.

Yeast

A fungi, which, given the right conditions, ferments, acting as a rising agent in dough.

Zest

The rind of a citrus fruit, removed by paring or grating and added to bread to give flavour.

USEFUL CONTACTS

Bakery Bits Ltd
7 Lowmoor Business Park
Tonedale
Wellington
Somerset
TA21 0AZ
Tel: 01404 565656
www.bakerybits.co.uk
Ingredients, equipment and courses.

Clyston Mill
Broadclyst
Exeter
EX5 3EW
Tel: 01392 462425
www.nationaltrust.org.uk
A watermill in a picturesque setting by
the River Clyst.

Cotehele Mill
Saint Dominic
Near Saltash
PL12 6TA
Tel: 01579 351346
www.nationaltrust.org.uk
Working Victorian watermill.

Doves Farm Ltd
Salisbury Road
Hungerford
Berkshire
RG17 0RF
Tel: 01488 684880
www.dovesfarm.co.uk

A selection of organic flour, including
heritage flour and gluten free, as well
as some baking equipment.

Electronic Temperature Instruments
Easting Close
Worthing
West Sussex
BN14 8HQ
Tel: 01903 202151
www.thermometer.co.uk
A digital thermometer manufacturer.

Heatherslaw Cornmill
Ford & Etal Estates
Heatherslaw
Cornhill-on-Tweed
Northumberland TD12 4TJ
Tel: 01890 820488
www.ford-and-etal.co.uk/heatherslaw-
mill
Working cornmill on the Ford & Etal
Estate.

Little Salkeld Watermill
The Watermill
Little Salkeld
Penrith
Cumbria
CA10 1NN
Tel: 01768 881523
www.organicmill.co.uk
Specialist millers of a broad range of
British grain.

LODE MILL
Quy Road
Lode
Cambridge
CB25 9EJ
Tel: 01223 810080
www.nationaltrust.org.uk
There has been a mill on this site for
around a thousand years. Most of the
working parts of the current mill are
about 150 years old.

Nisbets
Fourth Way
Avonmouth
Bristol
BS11 8TB
Tel: 01173 165000
www.nisbets.co.uk
Full range of catering equipment.

Shipton Mill Ltd
Long Newnton
Tetbury
Gloucestershire
GL8 8RP
Tel: 01666 505050
www.shipton-mill.com
Shipton Mill has been producing flour
since the time of the Domesday Book
and sells a range of flour, yeast and
baking equipment.

Stainsby Mill
Doe Lea
Chesterfield
Derbyshire
S44 5RW
Tel: 01246 850430

www.nationaltrust.org.uk
Situated on the Hardwick estate, the
mill offers a vivid evocation of the
workplace of a 19th-century miller.

Stoate & Sons
Cann Mills
Shaftesbury
Dorset
SP7 0BL
Tel: 01747 852475
www.stoatesflour.co.uk
A comprehensive range of organic and
non-organic flour.

Tintagel Old Post Office
Fore Street
Tintagel
Cornwall
PL34 0DB
Tel: 01840 770024
www.nationaltrust.org.uk

The Traditional Corn Millers Guild
www.tcmg.org.uk/
The TCMG's website lists traditional
mills around the UK enabling you to
source local freshly milled flour.

Winchester City Mill
Bridge Street
Winchester
Hampshire
SO23 9BH
Tel: 01962 870057
www.nationaltrust.org.uk
A water-mill in the heart of
Winchester.

Bibliography

Bailey, Adrian, *The Blessings of Bread*, Paddington Press Ltd, 1975

Baker, Gerard, *How to Avoid a Soggy Bottom*, Ebury Publishing, 2013

Balinska, Maria, *The Bagel*, Yale University Press, 2008

Cohen, W.L., *Baking Bread with Children*, Hawthorn Press, 2008

David, Elizabeth, *English Bread and Yeast Cookery*, Allen Lane, 1977

Freeman, Bobby, *A Book of Welsh Bread*, Y Lolfa Cyf, 1981

Hartley, Dorothy, *Food in England*, Macdonald, 1954

Hitz, Ciril, *Handmade Breads*, Apple Press, 2008

Hollywood, Paul, *100 Great Breads*, Cassell Illustrated, 2004

Mason, Jane, *All You Knead is Bread*, Ryland Peters and Small, 2012

Mayle, Peter, and Auzet, Gerard, *Confessions of a French Baker*,
Time Warner Books, 2005

McCance, R.A., and Widdowson, E.M., *Breads White and Brown*,
Pitman Medical Publishing Co Ltd, 1956

Norman, Ursel, *Use Your Loaf*, Fontana, 1976

Sheppard, Ronald, and Newton, Edward, *The Story of Bread*,
Routledge and Kegan Paul, 1957

Storck, John, and Dorwin Teague, Walter, *Flour for Man's Bread*,
University of Minnesota Press, 1952

Whitley, Andrew, *Bread Matters*, Fourth Estate, 2006

Yates, Annette, *Fresh Bread in the Morning from your Bread
Machine*, Right Way, 2003

Breads and Muffins, Transatlantic Press, 2010

Index

ACKNOWLEDGEMENTS

I am indebted to numerous friends who helped and supported me whilst writing this book, not least the brave souls who sampled innumerable breads and buns, some of which did not make the final cut! Gilly Cubitt, a far better baker than I, has been incredibly helpful, offering words of wisdom, practical advice and plenty of encouragement. Aaron Ogles determinedly sampled everything going, even recipes containing his personal bête noire – dried fruit – and who now claims to be converted to the charms of the currant, raisin and sultana.

My neighbour and great chum Lynn Linton helped me overcome my fear of deep-fat frying in the quest to produce the perfect doughnut, kindly lent me her mother's precious recipe books and sampled numerous baked goods, including one almighty disaster, for which I apologise profusely.

Dave Harris Jones, Head Miller at Heatherslaw Cornmill on the Ford & Etal Estates in Northumberland, very kindly read my copy and made some helpful suggestions. Sheila Connell, also a miller at Heatherslaw, came up with some useful points.

I must thank my daughter, Florence Eastoe, for her patient proof-reading, and my son Teddy for his kind outrage at missing the testing process while away at university. My husband, despite pleading gluten intolerance, has manfully sampled everything. He was uncomplaining when I turned the kitchen into a virtual branch of Greggs the bakers in the name of research, and remained tolerant when both wife and house vanished behind a haze of bread flour for many long months.

At the National Trust I would like to thank the many staff from various properties who so kindly scoured the archives looking for interesting recipes. Had space allowed I would have included many more of them, but in attempting to offer the reader a diverse selection I had to be ruthless in my editing. My apologies if your recipes did not make it, they all produced superb loaves and deserve to be reproduced.

At Pavilion I am continually thankful for the help and support of Polly Powell and my editors Peter Taylor and Cathy Gosling, and eternally grateful for their faith in me, and their patience and kindness.